1066

and All That

1066
and All That

W.C. SELLAR and R.J. YEATMAN

Introduction by FRANK MUIR

Line drawings by JOHN REYNOLDS

SUTTON PUBLISHING

First published in 1930 by Methuen & Co. Ltd

This illustrated edition first published in 1993 by
Alan Sutton Publishing Ltd, an imprint of
Sutton Publishing Limited
Phoenix Mill · Thrupp · Stroud · Gloucestershire · GL5 2BU

Reprinted in 1997, 1999

British Library Cataloguing in Publication Data

Sellar, W.C.
1066 and All That. – New ed.
I. Title II. Yeatman, R.J.
828.91207

ISBN 0-7509-1716-4

Front and back endpapers: Battle of Hastings, Bayeux Tapestry

Typeset in 10/12pt Imprint.
Typesetting and origination by
Sutton Publishing Limited.
Printed and bound in Great Britain by
Butler & Tanner, Frome, Somerset.

CONTENTS

'A Bad Queen'

ILLUSTRATIONS

DEDICATION

ABSIT OMAN

COMPULSORY PREFACE

(THIS MEANS YOU)

H ISTORIES have previously been written with the object of exalting their authors. The object of this History is to console the reader. *No other history does this.*

History is not what you thought. *It is what you can remember.* All other history defeats itself.

This is the only Memorable History of England, because all the History that you can remember is in this book, which is the result of years of research in golf-clubs, gun-rooms, green-rooms, etc.

For instance, 2 out of the 4 Dates originally included were eliminated at the last moment, a research done at the Eton and Harrow match having revealed that they are *not memorable*.

The Editors will be glad of further assistance towards the elimination, in future editions, of any similarly unhistorical matter which, despite their vigilance, may have crept into the text.

They take this opportunity of acknowledging their inestimable debt to the mass of educated men and women of their race whose historical intuitions and opinions this work enshrines.

Also, to the Great British People without whose self-sacrificing determination to become top Nation there would have been no (memorable) history.

History is now at an end (see p. 115); this History is therefore final.

W. C. S.
R. J. Y.

PREFACE TO SECOND EDITION

A FIRST edition limited to 1 copy and printed on rice paper and bound in buck-boards and signed by one of the editors was sold to the other editor, who left it in a taxi somewhere between Piccadilly Circus and the Bodleian.

W. C. S.
R. J. Y.

ACKNOWLEDGEMENTS

THE Editors acknowledge their comparative indebtedness to the Editors of *The Historical Review, Bradshaw, The Lancet, La Vie Parisienne*, etc., in which none of the following chapters has appeared. Their thanks are also due to their wife, for not preparing the index wrong. There is no index.

PRESS OPINIONS

'This slim volume . . .' (*The Bookworm*)

'. . . We look forward keenly to the appearance of their last work.' (*The Review of Reviews of Reviews*)

'. . . vague . . .' (*Vague*)

AUTHORS' NOTE

SEVERAL portions of this book have appeared in *Punch*, and are reprinted here by courtesy of the Proprietors of that paper.

ERRATA

p. 2 *For* Middletoe *read* Mistletoe.
p. 10 *For* looked 4th *read* looked forth.
p. 46 *For* Pheasant *read* Peasant, throughout.
p. 50 *For* sausage *read* hostage.

INTRODUCTION TO THIS EDITION

By Frank Muir

DURING the 1920s and 1930s, the now late and variously lamented magazine *Punch* was on what was to prove to be its last winning streak; it was then as good as it had ever been and was still the leading humorous journal by a mile at a time when there were something like twenty or thirty other comical magazines struggling to find a place in the sun.

Punch of the 1920s was very little different from *Punch* of the 1910s in spite of the Great War having happened in between. The younger blades had gone off to the war and the too-old-to-fight humorists who had replaced them for lunches round the *Punch* table were still round the table in the post-war '20s. It was not until late in the 1930s that the *New Yorker*'s influence on magazine humour was reluctantly acknowledged and *Punch* began to use brief captions underneath its joke cartoons instead of the usual four or five lines of dialogue, and Owen Seaman, the classicist and traditionalist editor, permitted brief excursions into the new American 'crazy humour' (referred to by Robert Benchley as the *dementia preacox* school).

Being the leading market for humour, *Punch* attracted submissions from ordinary readers all over the world who sent in odd paragraphs and funny misprints. 'Good enough for *Punch*' became a catchphrase, much used later by 'Beachcomber', and the magazine always featured a number of these non-fictional comic items:

MISTAKEN FOR RABBIT
Barking Girl Accidentally Shot

Body Found in River
The police are trying to establish the identity of the woman whose body has been recovered from the river above Chertsey, he told the committee, amid laughter.

The day's play had a result highly gratifying to Victorian golfers, for it placed on top of the list the girl champion of a year or two back. She appeared in something like her true colours, although her long shorts were not coming off with the desired regularity.

The magazine also attracted some of the best young professional writers to its staff. There was A.A. Milne whose verses *When We Were Very Young* were tremendously popular; and A.P. Herbert, the brilliant writer of witty verse and hard-hitting articles about almost everything. A.P.H.'s mock Law Reports, *Misleading Cases*, was one of *Punch*'s great series. In it he mocked asinine points of law, for example, when his hero Albert Haddock thought he was charged too much income tax, Haddock (quite legally) sent in his cheque written on a cow:

'Was the cow crossed?'
'No, your worship, it was an open cow.'

And, of course, the magazine attracted semi-professional humorists who had regular jobs outside journalism and wrote just for the fun of it or for the cachet of appearing in *Punch*.

Two spectacular examples of this very English way of going about things (although one of them was a Scot) were W.C. Sellar and R.J. Yeatman (Sellar was the Scot), the authors of one of the best-loved of all the English minor classics, *1066 and All That*.

They were an ill-assorted pair, it might be thought, to collaborate on a minor comic masterpiece. Walter Carruthers Sellar was born in Sutherland where his father farmed. He went to school at Fettes, near Edinburgh, became head boy and clearly was set on making teaching his career. He was a quiet lad with a melancholy streak but, as was often the case with deeply serious men, he took delight in Lear-like nonsense.

Robert Julian Yeatman on the other hand was witty and convivial. He was born in London but spent a great deal of time in Oporto in Portugal where the port comes from; his father was a wine-merchant (the family is still connected with Taylor's Port, i.e. Taylor, Fladgate and Yeatman Ltd). He was comfortably well-off and knocked about London with his fox-terrier, Jim, never more than about eight inches away from his right ankle – even at an audience with King George VI at a special royal performance of the stage version of *1066 and All That*; he painted, was a talented musician who could play almost any instrument, did some writing for films and seemed to know and be liked by everybody: when Clark Gable was filming in Britain he preferred to relax with the Yeatmans at their home rather than in his suite at the Connaught Hotel (Yeatman's son remembers one day watching Clark Gable stand in front of a mirror at their house, remove his dentures and murmur sadly, 'America's sweetheart!'

Walter Sellar and Julian Yeatman (which he pronounced 'Yetman') met for the first time at Oriel College, Oxford, just after the First World War. Both had fought and been wounded and at Oriel they began a lifelong friendship.

Sellar's wounds were only light but he suffered from poor health most of his life and died at the age of fifty-two.

Julian Yeatman, Military Cross, was severely wounded and so badly shot-up by shellfire that a friend said 'his body is perforated like a colander', but he continued to play strenuous sports during a long life.

When they came down from Oriel, Sellar became a teacher, as expected, and Yeatman got a job in the advertising

department of Kodak. A typical Yeatman contribution to Kodak's profits was his caption for one of the annual whole front-page ads in the *Daily Mail* at Easter. This featured a snapshot of a girl in a bathing costume clutching a lifebelt, beneath which Yeatman added:

> Girl meets buoy,
> Boy had a 'Kodak'.

During the early '20s they began, separately and together, submitting to *Punch* (anonymously in those days) deadpan, nonsensical little pieces, for example,

The Truth About Birds:

All birds are more or less brown, though adult swans are an exception. The only bird whose song can be identified for certain is the swan. This can be done by watching the bird singing: if the bird dies at the end then you know it was a swan.

Some Items of News Worth Knowing

MAN SWALLOWS MACKINTOSH. Amazing episode at Oxford Circus. The consumer was a middle-aged man with blue eyes and a small well-cropped moustache. When questioned by the policeman on point-duty the man stated that his name was Jones and that he was married and had a family of three daughters. 'The presence of a mackintosh in the alimentary tract', states a medical practitioner, 'sets up an irregular condition but not necessarily a fatal one. Cases of mackintosh craving have been rare in the British Isles in recent years.'

PRETTY GIRL'S ORDEAL.
Chased by Giant Shrimp. Mystery Rescuer.

CHILD SWIMMING PRODIGY TO ATTEMPT ATLANTIC.
Webbed Feet That Will Help
Mother Confident.

'Top nation'

The going rate in the early '20s for that kind of whimsy was £2.12s.0d. a paragraph, not really enough to keep two families going, particularly as Sellar had decided to take a few months away from schoolmastering (and a steady income) to try his hand at earning a living by writing.

The two men, still in their early twenties, set about devising a series for *Punch*. It was in a series that the money lay. And fame and everything else. The circulation of *Punch* took off for the first time when it published a series by Douglas Jerrold, *Mrs Caudle's Curtain Lectures* and the same thing happened to the *New Yorker* with Clarence Day's *Life With Father*.

Yeatman visited Sellar at the school where he was teaching and they met in London but most of their collaboration was conducted by letter. Yet in spite of this they came up with a brilliantly original idea which was not only perfect for *Punch* but was obviously exactly the stuff to make into a series and a book.

The idea, simple enough, was to write a number of pieces parodying history lessons as taught in school from history textbooks. The touch of genius came in their insistence that history really consists only of those names and dates and wars which are memorable; the rest, being forgotten, no longer exist. So they gave their book version a sub-title:

A Memorable History of England,
Comprising all the parts you can remember,
including 103 Good Things,
5 Bad Kings and
2 Genuine Dates

They began to exchange notes and ideas and when they met they drank a lot and shouted and it all went well, beginning its run in *Punch* in 1929. Perhaps the only real hiccough came when they had completed the book version; Yeatman left it in a taxi and they had to start again from the beginning. The book was published in 1930.

They went on to write three more comic works: *And Now All This*, *Horse Nonsense* (mainly by Yeatman, Sellar disliked horses) and *Garden Rubbish* (mainly by Sellar, Yeatman loathed gardening). These were good fun and contained a good many Sellar and Yeatman felicities (such as the comment in *Horse Nonsense*, 'One man's Meet is another man's poison' and a reminder that the horse is the only animal you can hammer nails into). But the sequels did not have the genius of the first book.

1066 was later made into a musical with lyrics by Reginald Arkell and with Naunton Wayne playing the part of the suave compere. It ran for many years.

Sellar and Yeatman's achievement was managing in *1066 and All That* to write only about those bits of history which almost every Britisher just about remembered, given a moment or two to think; those few names – like The Venerable Bede – and places – like Oudenard – and historical phrases – like 'ravaging the north' – which somehow penetrated the natural defences of schoolchildren and stayed in their memories.

And now here, over sixty years later, Sellar and Yeatman's *jeu d'esprit* blossoms yet again into print. The mad punning, the running jokes, the freshness and wit of the humour and its sheer exuberance now ensure its rightful place alongside *The Diary of a Nobody* and *Three Men in a Boat* as one of the permanent treasures of Eng. Lit. as Entertainment – And All That.

FRANK MUIR
1992

CHAPTER I

CAESAR INVADES BRITAIN

T HE first date* in English History is 55 BC in which year Julius Caesar (the *memorable* Roman Emperor) landed, like all other successful invaders of these islands, at Thanet. This was in the Olden Days, when the Romans were top nation on account of their classical education, etc.

Julius Caesar advanced very energetically, throwing his cavalry several thousands of paces over the River Flumen; but the Ancient Britons, though all well over military age, painted themselves true blue, or *woad*, and fought as heroically under their dashing queen, Woadicea, as they did later in thin red lines under their good queen, Victoria.

Julius Caesar was therefore compelled to invade Britain again the following year (54 BC, not 56, owing to the peculiar Roman method of counting), and having defeated the Ancient Britons by unfair means, such as battering-rams, tortoises, hippocausts, centipedes, axes and bundles, set the memorable Latin sentence, 'Veni, Vidi, Vici,' which the Romans, who were all very well educated, construed correctly.

The Britons, however, who of course still used the old pronunciation, understanding him to have called them 'Weeny, Weedy and Weaky', lost heart and gave up the struggle, thinking that he had already divided them All into Three Parts.

'Dawn of British heroism'

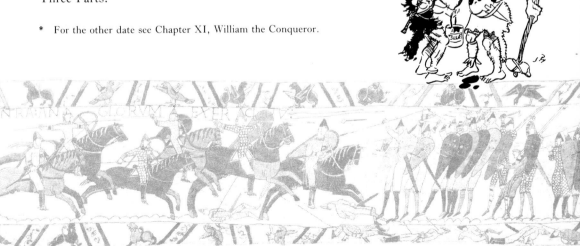

* For the other date see Chapter XI, William the Conqueror.

CULTURE AMONG THE ANCIENT BRITONS

The Ancient Britons were by no means savages before the Conquest, and had already made great strides in civilisation, e.g. they buried each other in long round wheelbarrows (agriculture) and burnt each other alive (religion) under the guidance of even older Britons called Druids and Eisteddfods, who worshipped the Middletoe in the famous Druidical churchyard at Stoke Penge.

The Roman Conquest was, however, a *Good Thing*, since the Britons were only natives at that time.

'Stoke Penge'

'Agriculture'

'They buried each other in wheelbarrows'

'The Roman Baths'

THE ROMAN OCCUPATION

For some reason the Romans neglected to overrun the country with fire and the sword, though they had both of these; in fact, after the Conquest they did not mingle with the Britons at all, but lived a semi-detached life in villas. They occupied their time for two or three hundred years in building Roman roads and having Roman baths; this was called the Roman Occupation, and gave rise to the memorable Roman law, 'HE WHO BATHS FIRST BATHS FAST,' which was a Good Thing, and still is. The Roman roads ran absolutely straight in all directions and all led to Rome. The Romans also built towns wherever they were wanted, and, in addition, a wall between England and Scotland to keep

'Roman occupied'

'The Picts, or painted men'

out the savage Picts and Scots. This wall was the work of the memorable Roman Emperor Balbus and was thus called Hadrian's Wall. The Picts, or painted men,* were so called to distinguish them from the Britons. (See *supra, woad*.)

* e.g. The Black Watch. The Red Comyn and Douglases of all colours.

CHAPTER II

BRITAIN CONQUERED AGAIN

THE withdrawal of the Roman legions to take part in Gibbon's Decline and Fall of the Roman Empire (due to a clamour among the Romans for pompous amusements such as bread and circumstances) left Britain defenceless and subjected Europe to that long succession of Waves of which History is chiefly composed. While the Roman Empire was overrun by waves not only of Ostrogoths, Visigoths and even Goths, but also of Vandals (who destroyed works of art) and Huns (who destroyed everything and everybody, including Goths, Ostrogoths, Visigoths and even Vandals), Britain was attacked by waves of Picts (and, of course, Scots) who had recently learnt how to climb the wall, and of Angles, Saxons and Jutes who, landing at Thanet, soon overran the country with fire (and, of course, the sword).

IMPORTANT NOTE

The Scots (originally Irish, but by now Scotch) were at this time inhabiting Ireland, having driven the Irish (Picts) out of Scotland; while the Picts (originally Scots) were now Irish (living in brackets) and *vice versa*. It is essential to keep these distinctions clearly in mind (and *verce visa*).

HUMILIATION OF THE BRITONS

The brutal Saxon invaders drove the Britons westward into Wales and compelled them to become Welsh; it is now considered doubtful whether this was a Good Thing. Memorable among the Saxon warriors were Hengist and his wife (? or horse), Horsa. Hengist made himself King in the South. Thus Hengist was the first English King and his wife (or horse), Horsa, the first English Queen (or horse). The country was now almost entirely inhabited by Saxons

'(? or horse)'

and was therefore renamed England, and thus (naturally) soon became C of E. This was a Good Thing, because previously the Saxons had worshipped some dreadful gods of their own called Monday, Tuesday, Wednesday, Thursday, Friday and Saturday.

'Angels?'

CHAPTER III

THE CONVERSION OF ENGLAND

NOTICING some fair-haired children in the slave market one morning, Pope Gregory, the memorable Pope, said (in Latin), 'What are those?' and on being told that they were Angels, made the memorable joke – 'Non Angli, sed Angeli' ('*not* Angels, but *Anglicans*') and commanded one of his saints called St Augustine to go and convert the rest.

The conversion of England was thus effected by the landing of St Augustine in Thanet and other places, which resulted in the country being overrun by a Wave of Saints. Among these were St Ive, St Pancra, the great St Bernard (originator of the clerical collar), St Bee, St Ebb, St Neot (who invented whisky), St Kit and St Kin, and the Venomous Bead (author of *The Rosary*).

England was now divided into seven kingdoms and so ready were the English to become C of E that on one memorable occasion a whole Kingdom was easily converted by a sparrow.

WAVE OF EGG-KINGS

Soon after this event Egg-Kings were found on the thrones of all these kingdoms, such as Eggberd, Eggbreth, Eggfroth, etc. None of them, however, succeeded in becoming memorable – except in so far as it is difficult to forget such names as Eggbirth, Eggbred, Eggbeard, Eggfilth, etc. Nor is it even remembered by what kind of Eggdeath they perished.

'Wave of Sts'

CHAPTER IV

BRITAIN CONQUERED AGAIN

THE conversion of Britain was followed by a Wave of Danes, accompanied by their sisters or *Sagas*, and led by such memorable warriors as Harold Falsetooth and Magnus the Great, who, landing correctly in Thanet, overran the country from right to left, with fire.*
After this the Danes invented a law called the Danelaw, which easily proved that since there was nobody else left alive there, all the right-hand part of England belonged to them. The Danish Conquest was, however, undoubtedly a *Good Thing*, because although it made the Danes top nation for a time it was the cause of Alfred the Cake (and in any case they were beaten utterly *in the end* by Nelson).

By this time the Saxons had all become very old like the Britons before them and were called *ealdormen*; when they had been defeated in a battle by the Danes they used to sing little songs to themselves such as the memorable fragment discovered in the Bodleian Library at Oxford:

OLD-SAXON FRAGMENT

Syng a song of Saxons
In the Wapentake of Rye
Four and twenty eaoldormen
Two eaold to die . . .

Anon

The Danes, on the other hand, wrote a very defiant kind of Epic poetry, e.g.:

BEOLEOPARD

. . . .

OR

THE WITAN'S WHAIL

. .

* And according to certain obstinate historians, the Sword.

'*Swingéd Cnut Cyng . . .*'

Whan Cnut Cyng the Witan wold enfeoff
Of infanthief and outfangthief
Wonderlich were they enwraged
And wordwar waged
Sware Cnut great scot and lot
Swingë wold ich this illbegotten lot.

Wroth was Cnut and wrothword spake.
Well wold he win at wopantake.
Fain wold he brakë frith and crackë heads
And than they shold worshippe his redes.

Swingéd Cnut Cyng with swung sword
Howléd Witanë hellë but hearkened his word
Murië sang Cnut Cyng
Outfangthief is Damgudthyng.

CHAPTER V

ALFRED THE CAKE

KING ALFRED was the first Good King, with the exception of Good King Wenceslas, who, though he looked 4th, really came first (it is not known, however, what King Wenceslas was King of). Alfred ought never to be confused with King Arthur, equally memorable but probably non-existent and therefore perhaps less important historically (unless he did exist).

There is a story that King Arthur once burnt some cakes belonging to Mrs Girth, a great lady of the time, at a place called Atheling. As, however, Alfred could not have been an Incendiary King *and* a Good King, we may dismiss the story as absurd, and in any case the event is supposed to have occurred in a marsh where the cakes would not have burnt properly. Cf. the famous lines of poetry about King Arthur and the cakes:

'Then slowly answered Alfred from the marsh – '

Arthur, Lord Tennyson

CHAPTER VI

EXGALAHAD AND THE BRITISH NAVY

KING ARTHUR invented Conferences because he was secretly a Weak King and liked to know what his memorable thousand and one Knights wanted to do next. As they were all parfitly jealous Knights he had to have the Memorable Round Table made to have the Conferences at, so that it was impossible to say which was top knight. He had a miraculous sword called Exgalahad with which he defeated the Danes in numerous battles. In this he was also much assisted by his marine inventions, including the water-clock and the British Navy. The latter invention occurred as follows.

'The Memorable Round Table'

Alfred noticed that the Danes had very long ships, so he built a great many more much longer ones, thus cleverly founding the British Navy. From that time onwards foreigners, who, unlike the English, do not prefer to fight against long odds, seldom attacked the British Navy. Hence the important International Law called the Rule Britannia, technically known as the Freedom of the Seas.

HUMILIATION OF THE DANES

The English resisted the Danes heroically under Alfred,

never fighting except against heavy odds, till at the memorable Peace of Wedmore Alfred compelled the Danes, who were now (of course) beaten, to stop being Danes and become English and therefore C of E and get properly married.

For this purpose they were made to go back and start again at Thanet, after which they were called in future Thanes instead of Danes and were on our side and in the right and very romantic.

CHAPTER VII

LADY WINDERMERE. AGE OF LAKE DWELLERS

ALFRED had a very interesting wife called Lady Windermere (The Lady of the Lake), who was always clothed in the same white frock, and used to go bathing with Sir Launcelot (also of the Lake) and was thus a Bad Queen. It was also in King Arthur's time that the *Anglo-Saxon Chronicle* was published: this was the first English newspaper and had all the news about his victories, and Lady Windermere, and the Cakes, etc.

CHAPTER VIII

ETHELREAD THE UNREADY, A WEAK KING

ETHELREAD THE UNREADY was the first Weak King of England and was thus the cause of a fresh Wave of Danes.

He was called the Unready because he was never ready when the Danes were. Rather than wait for him the Danes used to fine him large sums called Danegeld, for not being ready. But though they were always ready, the Danes had very bad memories and often used to forget that they had been paid the Danegeld and come back for it almost before they had sailed away. By that time Ethelread was always unready again.

'The first English newspaper'

Finally, Ethelred was taken completely unawares by his own death and was succeeded by Canute.

CHAPTER IX

CANUTE, AN EXPERIMENTAL KING

THIS memorable monarch, having set out from Norway to collect some Danegeld, landed by mistake at Thanet, and thus became King.

CANUTE AND THE WAVES

Canute began by being a Bad King on the advice of his Courtiers, who informed him (owing to a misunderstanding of the Rule Britannia) that the King of England was entitled to sit on the sea without getting wet. But finding that they were wrong he gave up this policy and decided to take his own advice in future – thus originating the memorable proverb, 'Paddle your own Canute' – and became a Good King and C of E, and ceased to be memorable. After Canute there were no more aquatic kings till William IV (see later, Creation of Piers).

Canute had two sons, Halfacanute and Partacanute, and two other offspring, Rathacanute and Hardlicanute, whom, however, he would never acknowledge, denying to the last that he was their Fathacanute.

CHAPTER X

EDWARD THE CONFESSOR

ON his death Canute's Kingdom was divided between two further sons, who had been previously overlooked. Aftercanute and Harold Harebrush. These were succeeded by Edward the Confessor. It was about this time that the memorable Mac Beth ('Ian Hay'), known as the Bane of Fife, murdered a number of his

*'Edward the Confessor
Perishes'*

enemies, including Mac Duff, Lord Dunsinaney, Sleep,
etc.

Edward the Confessor was with difficulty prevented
from confessing to all these and many other crimes committed in his reign, as he was in the habit of confessing
everything whether he had done it or not, and was thus a
Weak King.

THE LAST ENGLISH KING

With Edward the Confessor perished the last English King
(viz. Edward the Confessor), since he was succeeded by
Waves of Norman Kings (French), Tudors (Welsh),
Stuarts (Scottish) and Hanoverians (German), not to
mention the memorable Dutch King Williamanmary.

TEST PAPER I

UP TO THE END OF 1066

1. Which do you consider were the more alike, Caesar or Pompey, or *vice versa?* (Be brief.)

2. Discuss, in latin or gothic (*but not both*), whether the Northumbrian Bishops were more schismatical than the Cumbrian Abbots. (Be bright.)

3. Which came first, AD or BC? (Be careful.)

4. Has it never occurred to you that the Romans *counted backwards*? (Be honest.)

5. How angry would you be if it was suggested
   (1) That the XIth Chap, of the *Consolations of Boethius* was an interpolated palimpsest?
   (2) That an eisteddfod was an agricultural implement?

6. How would you have attempted to deal with
   (a) The Venomous Bead?
   (b) A Mabinogion or Wapentake? (Be quick.)

7. What would have happened if (*a*) Boadicea had been the daughter of Edward the Confessor? (*b*) Canute had succeeded in sitting on the waves?
   Does it matter?

8. Have you the faintest recollection of
   (1) Ethelbreth?
   (2) Athelthral?
   (3) Thruthelthrolth?

9. What *have* you the faintest recollection of?

10. Estimate the average age of
    (1) The Ancient Britons.
    (2) Ealdormen.
    (3) Old King Cole.

11. Why do you know nothing at all about
    (*a*) The Laws of Infangthief and Egg-seisin?
    (*b*) Saint Pancras?

12. Would you say that Ethelread the Unready was directly responsible for the French Revolution? If so, what *would* you say?

N.B. – Do not attempt to answer more than one question at a time.

CHAPTER XI

WILLIAM I, A CONQUERING KING

IN the year 1066 occurred the other memorable date in English History, viz. *William the Conqueror, Ten Sixty-six*. This is also called *The Battle of Hastings*, and was when William I (1066) conquered England at the Battle of Senlac (*Ten Sixty-six*).

When William the Conqueror landed he lay down on the beach and swallowed two mouthfuls of sand. This was his first conquering action and was in the South; later he ravaged the North as well.

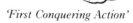

'First Conquering Action'

The Norman Conquest was a Good Thing, as from this time onwards England stopped being conquered and thus was able to become top nation.

DOOMSDAY BOOK AND THE FORESTS

William next invented a system according to which everybody had to belong to somebody else, and everybody else to the King. This was called the Feutile System, and in order to prove that it was true he wrote a book called the *Doomsday Book*, which contained an inventory of all the Possessions of all his subjects; after reading the book through carefully Williams agreed with it and signed it, indicating to everybody that the Possessions mentioned in it were now his.

William the Conqueror (1066) is memorable for having loved an old stag as if it was his father, and was in general very fond of animals: he therefore made some very just and conquering laws about the Forests. One of these laws said that *all the forests and places which were not already Possessions belonged to the King* and that anyone found in them should *have his ears and legs cut off* – (these belonged to somebody else under the Feutile System, anyway) – and (if his had not already been done) should have *his eyes put*

'The Battle of Hastings'

out with red-hot irons; after this the offender was allowed to fly the country.

Another very conquering law made by William I said that everyone had to go to bed at eight o'clock. This was called the Curfew and was a Good Thing in the end since it was the cause of Gray's Energy in the country churchyard (at Stoke Penge).

Although in all these ways William the Conqueror (1066) was a very strong king he was eventually stumbled to death by a horse and was succeeded by his son Rufus.

CHAPTER XII

RUFUS, A RUDDY KING

THIS monarch was always very angry and red in the face and was therefore unpopular, so that his death was a Good Thing: it occurred in the following memorable way. Rufus was hunting one day in the New Forest, when William Tell (the memorable crackshot,

'A Good Thing'

Cibabis nos pane lacrimarum: et
potum dabis nobis in lacrimis in

'The memorable crackshot'

inventor of Cross-bow puzzles) took unerring aim at a
reddish apple, which had fallen on to the King's head, and
shot him through the heart. Sir Isaac Walton, who happened to be present at the time, thereupon invented the
Law of Gravity. Thus was the reign of Rufus brought to a
Good End.

CHAPTER XIII

HENRY I, A TRAGIC KING

HENRY I was famous for his handwriting and was
therefore generally called Henry Beau-geste. He
was extremely fond of his son William, who was,
however, drowned in the White City. Henry tried to console

himself for his loss by eating a surfeit of palfreys. This was a Bad Thing since he died of it and *never smiled again*.

CHAPTER XIV

THE DREADFUL STORY OF STEPHEN AND HIS AUNT MATILDA (OR MAUD)

T HE moment Stephen came to the throne it was realised that he was a mistake and had been christened wrong; thus everything was thrown into confusion.

Stephen himself felt quite uncalled for, and even his Aunt Matilda was able to take him in when she began announcing that she was the real King. Stephen, however, soon discovered that she had been malchristened, too, and was unable to say for certain whether her name was Matilda or Maud.

After this Stephen and Matilda (or Maud) spent the reign escaping from each other over the snow in nightgowns while 'God and His Angels slept'.

Taking advantage of this lax state of affairs, the Barons built a surfeit of romantic castles, into which they lured everybody and then put them to the torture; nor is it recorded that the Sword was once sheathed, right to the bottom, during the whole of this dreadful reign. Hence the memorable greeting so common among the Barons of the time – 'Merrie Englande!'

CHAPTER XV

HENRY II, A JUST KING

H ENRY II was a great Lawgiver, and it was he who laid down the great Legal Principle that everything is either legal or (preferably) illegal.

He also made another very just arrangement about trials. Before Henry II's time there were two kinds of legal trial, (*a*) the Ideal and (*b*) the Combat. The Ideal form of trial

'Drowned in the White City'

'The dreadful story of Stephen'

consisted in making a man plunge his head in boiling ploughshares, in order to see whether he had committed a crime or not. According to Henry's reformed system a man was tried first by a jury of his equals and only had to plunge his head into the ploughshares afterwards (in order to confirm the jury's opinion that he had committed the crime). This was obviously a much *Better Thing*.

The Combat was a system by which in civil cases the litigants decided their dispute by mortal combat, after which the defeated party was allowed to fly the country. But Henry altered all this and declared that a Grand Jury must

decide first what the parties were fighting about: a reform which naturally gave rise to grave discontent among the Barons, who believed in the Combat, the whole Combat and nothing but the Combat.

'The Combat, the whole Combat and nothing but the Combat'

'Murdered him in the organ'

THOMAS À BELLOC

It was at this time that Thomas à Belloc, the great religious leader, claimed that clergymen, whatever crimes they might commit, could not be punished at all; this privilege, which was for some reason known as Benefit of Clergy, was in full accord with the devout spirit of the age. Henry II, however, exclaimed to some of his Knights one day 'Who will rid me of this Chesterton beast?' Whereupon the Knights pursued Belloc and murdered him in the organ at Canterbury Cathedral. Belloc was therefore made a Saint and the Knights came to be called the Canterbury Pilgrims.

Shortly afterwards Henry died of despair on receiving news that his sons were all revolting.

CHAPTER XVI

THE AGE OF PIETY

THE Chapters between William I (1066) and the Tudors (Henry VIII, etc.) are always called the *Middle Ages*, on account of their coming at the beginning; this was also *The Age of Piety*, since Religious fervour was then at its height, people being (1) burnt alive with faggots (The Steak), (2) bricked up in the walls of Convents (Religious Foundations) and (3) tortured in dungeons (The Confessional).

All this was not only pious but a Good Thing, as many of the people who were burnt, bricked, tortured, etc., became quite otherwordly.

'Burnt alive with faggots (The Steak)'

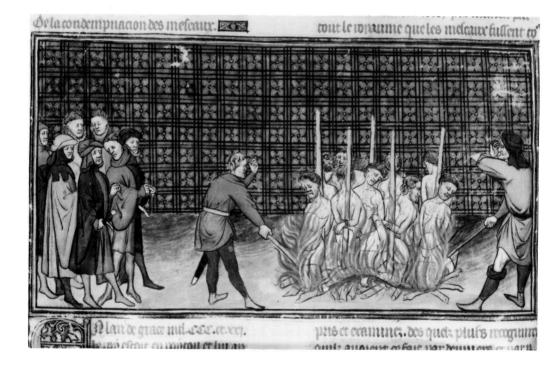

Nowadays people are not so pious, even heretics being denied the benefits of fervent Religion.

CHAPTER XVII

RICHARD I, A WILD KING

RICHARD I was a hairy King with a Lion's Heart; he went roaring about the Desert making ferocious attacks on the Saladins and the Paladins, and was thus a very romantic King. Whenever he returned to England he always set out again immediately for the Mediterranean and was therefore known as Richard Gare de Lyon. He had a sword of enormous dimensions with which he used to practise cutting iron bars and anvils in half, whereas the Saladins had very sharp swords which were only useful for cutting cushions in half. In spite of which the Crusaders under Richard never got Jerusalem back: this was undoubtedly due to the treacherous behaviour of the Saladins, who used to fire on the Red Cross which the Crusaders wore on their chests in battle.

'*A Wild King*'

THE STORY OF BLONDIN

Richard is also famous for having a minstrel boy (or Touralour) called Blondin who searched for him under the walls of the dungeons in Europe. This was when Richard had been caught by the blind King of Bohemia during a game of Blind King's Bluff and sold to the Holy Roman Terror. Blondin eventually found him by singing the memorable song (or 'touralay') called 'O Richard et mon Droit' ('Are you right, there, Richard?'), which Richard himself had composed. Richard roared the chorus so that Blondin knew which dungeon he was in, and thus the King easily escaped and returned to the Crusades, where he died soon after of a surfeit of Saladins, and was therefore known in the East as Richard Coeur de Laitue.

CHAPTER XVIII

JOHN, AN AWFUL KING

WHEN John came to the throne he lost his temper and flung himself on the floor, foaming at the mouth and biting the rushes. He was thus a Bad King. Indeed, he had begun badly as a Bad Prince, having attempted to answer the Irish Question* by pulling the beards of the aged Irish chiefs, which was a Bad Thing and the wrong answer.

PRINCE ARTHUR – A TRAGEDY IN LITTLE

John had a little nephew called Little Arthur, who was writing a little History of England in quite a small dungeon, and whose little blue eyes John had ordered to be put out with some weeny red-hot irons. The gaoler Hubert, however, who was a Good Man, wept so much that he put out the red-hot irons instead. John was therefore compelled to do the little deed himself with a large, smallish knife, thus becoming the first memorable wicked uncle.

THE BULL

John was so bad that the Pope decided to put the whole country under an Interdict, i.e. he gave orders that no one was to be born or die or marry (except in Church porches). But John was still not cured of his Badness; so the Pope sent a Bull to England to excommunicate John himself. In spite of the King's efforts to prevent it the Bull succeeded in landing and gave orders that John himself was not to be born or marry or die (except in Church porches); that no one was to obey him or stand him a drink or tell him the

'No one was to marry (except in church porches)'

---

* N.B. – The Irish Question at this time consisted of:
      (1) Some Norman Barons, who lived in a Pail (near Dublin).
      (2) The natives and Irish Chieftains, who were beyond the Pail, living in bogs, beards, etc.

'The Bull succeeded in landing in England'

right time or the answer to the Irish Question or anything nice. So at last John gave way and he and his subjects began once more to be born and to marry and to die, etc. etc.

CHAPTER XIX

MAGNA CHARTER

THERE also happened in this reign the memorable Charta, known as Magna Charter on account of the Latin *Magna* (great) and Charter (a Charter); this was the first of the famous Chartas and Gartas of the Realm and was invented by the Barons on a desert island in the Thames called Ganymede. By congregating there, armed to the teeth, the Barons compelled John to sign the Magna Charter, which said:

1. That no one was to be put to death, save for some reason – (except the Common People).
2. That everyone should be free – (except the Common People).
3. That everything should be of the same weight and measure throughout the Realm – (except the Common People).
4. That the Courts should be stationary, instead of following a very tiresome medieval official known as the *King's Person* all over the country.
5. That 'no person should be fined to his utter ruin' – (except the King's Person).
6. That the Barons should not be tried except by a special jury of other Barons who would understand.

Magna Charter was therefore the chief cause of Democracy in England, and thus a *Good Thing* for everyone (except the Common People).

After this King John hadn't a leg to stand on and was therefore known as 'John Lackshanks'.

FINAL ACTS OF MISGOVERNMENT

John finally demonstrated his utter incompetence by losing the Crown and all his clothes in the wash and then dying of a surfeit of peaches and no cyder; thus his awful reign came to an end.

CHAPTER XX

'*Utter Incompetence*'

ROBIN HOOD AND HIS MERRIE MEN

ABOUT this time the memorable hero Robin Hood flourished in a romantic manner. Having been unjustly accused by two policemen in Richmond Park, he was condemned to be an outdoor and went and lived with a maid who was called Marion, and a band of Merrie Men, in Greenwood Forest, near Sherborne.

'*Robin Hood spent his time blowing a horn and shooting at the Sheriff of Nottingham (who was an outwit)*'

Amongst his Merrie Men were Will Scarlet (*The Scarlet Pimpernel*), Black Beauty, White Melville, Little Red Riding Hood (probably an outdaughter of his) and the famous Friar Puck who used to sit in a cowslip and suck bees, thus becoming so fat that he declared he could put his girdle round the Earth.

Robin Hood was a miraculous shot with the longbow and it is said that he could split a hare at 400 paces and a Sheriff at 800. He therefore spent his time blowing a horn and shooting at the Sheriff of Nottingham (who was an outwit). He always used to sound his horn first, particularly when shooting round a corner; this showed his sportsmanship and also enabled him to shoot the Sheriff running, which was more difficult.

Robin Hood was also very good at socialism and often took money away from rich clergymen and gave it to the poor, who loved him for his generosity. He died very

romantically. Having taken some medicine supplied by his Wicked Aunt and feeling his strength going, he blew a dying blast on his horn and with his dying breath fired a last shot out of his bedroom window, and *hit the Sheriff of Nottingham again.*

CHAPTER XXI

HENRY III, A NONDESCRIPT KING

HENRY III was a confused kind of King and is only memorable for having seized all the money in the Mint, imprisoned himself in the Tower of London and, finally, flung himself into the Bosom of the Pope.

While he was in the Tower, Henry III wrote a letter to the nation saying that he was a Good Thing. This so confused the Londoners that they armed themselves with staves, jerkins, etc., and massacred the Jews in the City. Later, when he was in the Pope's Bosom, Henry further confused the People by presenting all the Bonifaces of the Church to Italians. And the whole reign was rapidly becoming less and less memorable when one of the Barons

'Massacred the Jews'

called Simon de Montfort saved the situation by announcing that he had a memorable idea.

SIMON DE MONTFORT'S GOOD IDEA

Simon de Montfort's idea was to make the Parliament more Representative by inviting one or two vergers, or vergesses, to come from every parish, thus causing the only Good Parliament in History.

THE BARONS

Simon de Montfort, though only a Frenchman, was thus a Good Thing, and is very notable as being the only good Baron in history. The other Barons were, of course, all wicked Barons. They had, however, many important duties under the Banorial system. These were:

1. To be armed to the teeth.
2. To extract from the Villein* Saccage and Soccage, tollage and tallage, pillage and ullage, and, in extreme cases, all other banorial amenities such as umbrage and porrage. (These may be collectively defined as the banorial rites of carnage and wreckage).
3. To hasten the King's death, deposition, insanity, etc., and make quite sure that there were always at least three false claimants to the throne.
4. To resent the Attitude of the Church. (The Barons were secretly jealous of the Church which they accused of encroaching on their rites – see p. 24, Age of Piety.)
5. To keep up the Middle Ages.

NOTE

In order to clear up the general confusion of the period it is

'*To extract from the Villein*'

* Villein: medieval term for agricultural labourer, usually suffering from scurvy, Black Death, etc.

'The only Good Parliament in history'

customary to give at this point a genealogical table of the Kings (and even some Queens) of England. As these tables are themselves somewhat confusing, the one which follows has been to a certain extent *rationalized*, and will, the Editors hope, prove to be exceptionally memorable.

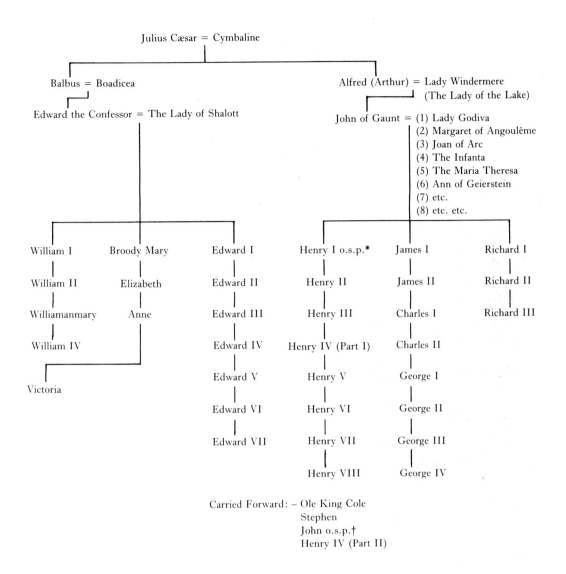

Julius Cæsar = Cymbaline

Balbus = Boadicea

Edward the Confessor = The Lady of Shalott

Alfred (Arthur) = Lady Windermere
(The Lady of the Lake)

John of Gaunt = (1) Lady Godiva
(2) Margaret of Angoulême
(3) Joan of Arc
(4) The Infanta
(5) The Maria Theresa
(6) Ann of Geierstein
(7) etc.
(8) etc. etc.

William I	Broody Mary	Edward I	Henry I o.s.p.*	James I	Richard I
William II	Elizabeth	Edward II	Henry II	James II	Richard II
Williamanmary	Anne	Edward III	Henry III	Charles I	Richard III
William IV		Edward IV	Henry IV (Part I)	Charles II	
Victoria		Edward V	Henry V	George I	
		Edward VI	Henry VI	George II	
		Edward VII	Henry VII	George III	
			Henry VIII	George IV	

Carried Forward: – Ole King Cole
Stephen
John o.s.p.†
Henry IV (Part II)

* obiit surfeiti palfreyorum (see p. 19)
† peaches.

E. & O. E.

TEST PAPER II

UP TO THE END OF HENRY III

*1. Give the dates of at least two of the following
   (1) William the Conqueror.
   (2) 1066.
*2. What is a Plantagenet? Do you agree?
*3. Trace by means of graphs, etc.,
   (1) The incidence of scurvy in the Chiltern Hundreds during the reign of Rufus.
   (2) The Bosom of the Pope.
      (Squared paper, compasses, etc., may be used.)
*4. Expostulate (chiefly) on
   (a) The Curfew.
   (b) Gray's Energy in the Country Churchyard.
*5. Estimate the size of
   (1) Little Arthur.
   (2) Friar Puck.
   (3) Magna Charta.
 6. Fill in the names of at least some of the following:
   (1) ——.
   (2) ——.
   (3) Simon de Montfort.
 7. King John had no redeeming features. (Illustrate.)
 8. Arrange in this order:
   (1) Henry I.
   (2) Henry II.
   (3) Henry III.
   (Do not attempt to answer more than once.)
*9. (a) How far did the Lords Repellent drive Henry III into the arms of Pedro the Cruel? (Protractors may not be used.)
   (b) Matilda or Maud? (Write on one side of the paper only.)
*10. How would you dispose of
   (a) A Papal Bull?
   (b) Your nephews?
   (c) Your mother? (Be brutal.)
*11. Which would you rather be
   (1) The Sheriff of Nottingham?
   (2) A Weak King?
   (3) Put to the Sword?

*N.B. – Candidates over thirty need not attempt questions 10, 2, 5, 3, 4, 11, 9 or 1.

CHAPTER XXII

EDWARD I, A STRONG KING

LONG before Henry III had died (of a surfeit of Barons, Bonifaces, etc.) Edward I had taken advantage of the general confusion and of the death of Simon de Montfort (probably of a surfeit of Vergers) to become King before his reign had begun.

Edward I was thus a strong King, and one of the first things he did was to make a strong arrangement about the Law Courts. Hitherto there had been a number of Benches there, on all of which a confused official called the Justinian had tried to sit. Edward had them all amalgamated into one large Bench called the King's Bench, and sat on it himself.

'Sat on it himself'

Edward I, who had already (in his Saladin days) piously decimated several thousand Turks at Nazareth, now felt so strong that he decided to Hammer the Scots, who accordingly now come right into History.

The childless Scotch King Alexander the Great had trotted over a cliff and was thus dead; so the Scots asked Edward to tell them who was King of Scotland, and Edward said that a Balliol man ought to be. Delighted with this decision the Scots crossed the Border and ravaged Cumberland with savage ferocity; in reply to which Edward also crossed the Border and, carrying off the Sacred Scone of Scotland on which the Scottish Kings had been crowned for centuries, buried it with great solemnity in Westminster Abbey.

'Malleus Scotorum'

This was, of course, a Good Thing for the Scots because it was the cause of William the Wallace (not to be confused with Robert Bruce), who immediately defeated the English at Cambuskenneth (Scotch for Stirling) and invaded England with ferocious savagery. In answer to this Edward captured the Bruce and had him horribly executed with savage ferocity. Soon after, Edward died of suffocation at a place called Burrow-in-the-Sands and was succeeded by his worthless son Edward II.

'Trotted over a cliff'

CHAPTER XXIII

EDWARD II, A WORTHLESS KING

EDWARD II had a wave of favourites or hangers-on at Court, of whom the worst were the Suspenders and the Peers Gaveston. There were two memorable Suspenders, the Old Suspender and the Young Suspender and they were Edward's reply to the continual applications of the Barons for a confirmation of all the charters and garters of the Realm. But even Edward II's worthless character cannot alone explain. [*Sic*]

THE BATTLE OF BANNOCKBURN

The Scots were now under the leadership of the Bruce (not to be confused with the Wallace), who, doubtful whether he had slain the Red Comyn or not, armed himself with an enormous spider and marched against the English, determined if possible to win back the Great Scone by beating the English three times running.

The fact that the English were defeated has so confused Historians that many false theories are prevalent about the Bannockburn Campaign. What actually happened is quite clear from the sketch map which follows:

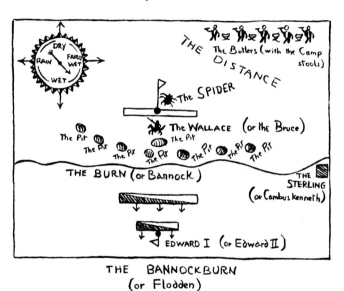

THE   BANNOCKBURN
(or Flodden)

The causes of the English defeat were all unfair and were:

1. *The Pits*. Every time the Wallace saw some English Knights charging at him he quickly dug one of these unnatural hazards into which the English Knights,

who had been taught to ride straight, galloped with flying colours.

2. *Superior numbers of the English* (four to one). Accustomed to fight against heavy odds the English were uneasy, and when the Scots were unexpectedly reinforced by a large body of butlers with camp stools the English soldiers mistook them for a fresh army of Englishmen and retreated in disgust.

3. *Foul riding by Scottish Knights.* This was typified even before the battle during an exhibition combat between the Bruce and the English Champion, Baron Henry le Bohunk, when Bruce, mounted on a Shetland pony, galloped underneath the Baron and, coming up unexpectedly on the blind side, struck him a foul blow behind and maced him up for life.

MEMORABLE SCREAMS OF EDWARD II

Edward II was so weak that he kept banishing his favourites and then unbanishing them again. The Barons therefore became so impatient that they deposed Edward without even waiting to arrange for any false claimants to the throne. Thus Edward III became King.

Shortly afterwards HORRIBLE SCREAMS were heard issuing from the Berkeley where Edward II was imprisoned and the next day he was horribly dead. But since not even the Barons would confess to having horribly murdered him, it is just possible that Edward had merely been dying of a surfeit in the ordinary way.

CHAPTER XXIV

EDWARD III, A ROMANTIC KING

EDWARD III had a very romantic reign which he began by confining his mother in a stronghold for the rest of her life, and inventing a law called the Gallic Law according to which he was King of France, and

'The Berkeley'

'Foul riding by Scottish Knights . . . maced him up for life'

could therefore make war on it whenever he felt inclined.

In order to placate Edward, the French King sent him a box of new tennis balls. When the parcel was opened the Prince of Wales, who was present, mottoed to himself memorably (in Bohemian) 'Ich Dien,' which means

'My serve,' and immediately invaded France with an army of archers. This prince was the memorable All-Black Prince, and the war was called the Hundred Years War, because the troops signed on for a hundred years or the duration.

'Immediately invaded France'

'The Battle of Cresy'

THE BATTLE OF CRESY

This decisive battle of the world was fought during a total eclipçe of the sun and naturally ended in a complete victory for the All-Black Prince, who very romantically 'won his Spurs'* by slaughtering one-third of the French nobility.

* His father the King had betted him a pair of hotspurs that he could not do this.

THE SIX BURGLARS OF CALAIS

Edward III then laid siege to Calais in order to be ready to return to England if necessary, and on the capitulation of the town ordered the six richest citizens to come forth with halters round their necks and wearing only their shorts, and to surrender all the keys in the city. The inhabitants therefore at once appointed the six chief burglars of Calais and Edward agreed with this, romantically commanding that they should be put to death as soon as they came in. His Queen, however, pointed out what a much more romantic thing it would be to pardon them and make them barons in the Exchequer. Edward therefore pardoned them in spite of his private feelings that the original plan was more romantic still.

After this Edward had all the wool in England kept in a stable at Calais instead of in a sack in the House of Commons; this was a Bad Thing, as it was the beginning of Political Economy.

WYCLIF AND THE DULLARDS

During this reign the memorable preacher Wyclif collected together a curious set of men known as the Lollards or Dullards, because they insisted on walking about with their tongues hanging out and because they were so stupid that

they could not do the Bible in Latin and demanded that everyone should be allowed to use an English translation. They were thus heretics and were accordingly unpopular with the top men in the Church who were very good at Latin and who liked to see some Dullards burnt before every meal. Hence the memorable grace 'De Heretico Comburendo, Amen,' known as the Pilgrim's Grace.

ROYAL TACT

Edward III had very good manners. One day at a royal dance he noticed some men-about-court mocking a lady whose garter had come off, whereupon to put her at her ease he stopped the dance and made the memorable epitaph: *'Honi soie qui mal y pense'* ('Honey, your silk stocking's hanging down') and having replaced the garter with a romantic gesture gave the ill-mannered courtiers the Order of the Bath. (This was an extreme form of torture in the Middle Ages.)

CHAPTER XXV

RICHARD II, AN UNBALANCED KING

RICHARD II was only a boy at his accession: one day, however, suspecting that he was now twenty-one, he asked his uncle and, on learning that he was, mounted the throne himself and tried first being a Good King and then being a Bad King, without enjoying either very much: then, being told that he was unbalanced, he got off the throne again in despair, exclaiming gloomily: 'For God's sake let me sit on the ground and tell bad stories about cabbages and things.' Whereupon his cousin Lancaster (spelt Bolingbroke), quickly mounted the throne and said he was Henry IV, Part I.

'Got off the throne'

Richard was thus abdicated and was led to the Tower and subsequently to Pontefract Castle where he died of mysterious circumstances, probably a surfeit of Pumfreys (spelt Pontefracts).

'The Order of the
Bath'

'Richard II tried first being a good king . . .'

APPENDIX

THE PHEASANTS REVOLT

They did this in several reigns under such memorable leaders as Black Kat, Straw Hat, John Bull and What Tyler?

'. . . then a bad king . . . He was led to the Tower'

I. Objects:
   (*a*) to obtain a free pardon for having revolted.
   (*b*) to find out which was the gentleman when Adam delved and Eve span. (The answer was, of course, Adam, but the mystics of the Church had concealed this dangerous knowledge.)
   (*c*) to find out who was King and which of them was the Leader of the Rebellion.
   (*d*) to abolish the Villein.

The Pheasants' Revolts were therefore purely educational movements and were thus easily suppressed.

II. How Quelled:
  (*a*) the Pheasants were met at Smithfield by the King who
  (*b*) riding forward alone on a white horse answered object (*c*) by announcing (I) 'I am your King', and (II) 'I will be your leader'.
  (*c*) the real leader was then slain quickly by one of the Barons.
  (*d*) a free pardon was granted to the Pheasants [see object (*a*)].
  (*e*) all were then put to death on the ground that they were Villeins [see object (*d*)].

These Revolts were thus clearly romantic episodes and a Good Thing, and the clergy were enabled to prevent the pheasants finding out the answer to object (*b*).

'The Pheasants met at Smithfield'

CHAPTER XXVI

HENRY IV, A SPLIT KING

WHEN Henry IV Part I came to the throne the Barons immediately flung their gloves on the floor in order to prove

1. That Richard II was not yet dead.
2. That Henry had murdered him.

'Henry had murdered him'

Henry very gallantly replied to this challenge by exhibiting Richard II's head in St Paul's Cathedral, thus proving that he was innocent. Finding, however, that he was not memorable, he very pathetically abdicated in favour of Henry IV, Part II.

RENEWED EDUCATIONAL FERMENT

Even Henry IV, Part II, however, is only memorable for having passed some interesting laws against his *Old Retainers*, i.e. butlers and sutlers, who had irritated him by demanding *Liveries*, requiring too much *Maintenance*, etc. He also captured the Scottish Prince James and, while keeping him as a sausage, had him carefully educated for nineteen years; finding, however, that James was still Scotch, Henry IV Part II lost interest in education and died.

CHAPTER XXVII

HENRY V, AN IDEAL KING

ON the death of Henry IV Part II, his son, Prince Hal, who had won all English hearts by his youthful pranks – (such as trying on the crown while his father lay dying, and hitting a very old man called Judge Gascoigne) – determined to justify public expectation by becoming the *Ideal English King*. He therefore decided on an immediate appearance in the Hundred Years War, making a declaration that all the treaties with France were to be regarded as dull and void.

Conditions in France were favourable to Henry since the French King, being mad, had entrusted the government of the country to a dolphin and the command of the army to an elderly constable. After capturing some breeches at Harfleur (more than once) by the original expedients of disguising his friends as imitation tigers, stiffening their sinews, etc, Henry was held up on the road to Calais by the constable, whom he

'The utterly memorable battle of Agincourt'

defeated at the utterably memorable battle of AGINCOURT (French POICTIERS). He then displaced the dolphin as ruler of Anjou, Menjou, Poilou, Maine, Touraine, Againe and Againe, and realising that he was now too famous to live long expired at the ideal moment.

CHAPTER XXVIII

HENRY VI, A VERY SMALL KING

THE next King, Henry VI, was only one year old and was thus rather a Weak King; indeed the Barons declared that he was quite numb and vague. When he grew up, however, he was such a Good

'A Weak King'

Man that he was considered a Saint, or alternatively (especially by the Barons) an imbecile.

JOAN OF ARK

During this reign the Hundred Years War was brought to an end by *Joan of Ark*, a French descendant of Noah who after hearing Angel voices singing *Do Ré Mi* became inspired, thus unfairly defeating the English in several battles. Indeed, she might even have made France top nation if the Church had not decided that she would make an exceptionally memorable martyr. Thus Joan of Ark was a Good Thing in the end and is now the only memorable French saint.

'A Good Thing'

THE WARS OF THE ROSES

Noticing suddenly that the Middle Ages were coming to an
end, the Barons now made a stupendous effort to revive the
old Feudal amenities of Sackage, Carnage and Wreckage
and so stave off the Tudors for a time. They achieved this
by a very clever plan, known as the *Wars of the Roses*
(because the Barons all picked different coloured roses in
order to see which side they were on).

WARWICK THE KINGMAKER

One of the rules in the Wars of the Roses was that nobody
was ever really King but that Edmund Mortimer really
ought to be: any Baron who wished to be considered King
was allowed to apply at Warwick the Kingmaker's, where he
was made to fill up a form, answering the following
questions:

1. Are you a good plain crook?
2. Are you Edmund Mortimer? If not, have you got
    him?
3. Have you ever been King before? If so, state how
    many times; also whether deposed, beheaded, or died
    of surfeit.
4. Are you insane? If so, state whether permanently or
    only temporarily.
5. Are you prepared to marry Margaret of Angoulême?
    If Isabella of Hainault preferred, give reasons. (Can-
    didates are advised not to attempt both ladies.)
6. Have you had the Black Death?
7. What have you done with your mother? (If *Nun*,
    write *None*.)
8. Do you intend to be   I   (*a*)   a Good King.
                              (*b*)   a Bad King.
                              (*c*)   a Weak King.
                         II   (*a*)   a Good Man.
                              (*b*)   a Bad Man.

(Candidates must not attempt more than one in each section.)

9. How do you propose to die? (Write your answer in BLOCK CAPITALS.)

CHAPTER XXIX

CAUSE OF THE TUDORS

'*Finding that his name was Clarence*'

DURING the Wars of the Roses the Kings became less and less memorable (sometimes even getting in the wrong order) until at last one of them was nothing but some little princes smothered in the Tower, and another, finding that his name was Clarence, had himself drowned in a spot of Malmsey wine; while the last of all even attempted to give his Kingdom to a horse. It was therefore decided, since the Stuarts were not ready yet, to have some Welsh Kings called Tudors (on account of their descent from Owen Glendower) who, it was hoped, would be more memorable.

The first of these Welsh Kings was Henry VII, who defeated all other Kings at the Battle of Boswell Field and took away their roses. After the battle the crown was found hanging up in a hawthorn tree on top of a hill. This is memorable as being the only occasion on which the crown has been found after a battle hanging up in a hawthorn tree on top of a hill.

HENRY VII'S STATECRAFT

Henry VII was a miser and very good at statecraft; he invented some extremely clever policies such as the one called Morton's Fork. This was an enormous prong with which his minister Morton visited the rich citizens (or burghlers as they were called). If the citizen said he was poor, Morton drove his Fork in a certain distance and promised not to take it out until the citizen paid a large sum of money to the King. As soon as this was forthcoming

'Henry VII . . . who took
away their roses'

Morton dismissed him, at the same time shouting 'Fork Out' so that Henry would know the statecraft had been successful. If the burghler said he was quite rich Morton did the same thing: it was thus a very clever policy and always succeeded, except when Morton put the Fork in too far.

'A certain distance'

CHAPTER XXX

LAMBERT SIMNEL AND PERKIN WARBECK

ENGLISH History has always been subject to Waves of Pretenders. These have usually come in small waves of about 2 – an Old Pretender and a Young Pretender, their object being to sow dissension in the realm, and if possible to confuse the Royal issue by pretending to be heirs to the throne.

Two Pretenders who now arose were Lambert Simnel and Perkin Warbeck and they succeeded in confusing the issue absolutely by being so similar that some historians suggest they were really the same person (i.e. the Earl of Warbeck).

Lambert Simnel (the Young Pretender) was really (probably) himself, but cleverly pretended to be the Earl of Warbeck. Henry VII therefore ordered him to be led through the streets of London to prove that he really was.

Perkin Warbeck (the Older and more confusing Pretender) insisted that he was himself, thus causing complete dissension till Henry VII had him led through the streets of London to prove that he was really Lambert Simnel.

'Punishment of Lamnel (or Wermkin)'

The punishment of these memorable Pretenders was justly simnilar, since Perkin Warmnel was compelled to become a blot on the King's skitchen, while Perbeck was made an escullion. Wimneck, however, subsequently began pretending again. This time he pretended that he had been smothered in early youth and buried under a stair-rod while pretending to be one of the Little Princes in the Tower. In

'Perkin Warbeck'

order to prove that he had not been murdered before, Henry was reluctantly compelled to have him really executed.

Even after his execution many people believed that he was only pretending to have been beheaded, while others declared that it was not Warmneck at all but Lamkin, and that Permnel had been dead all the time really, like Queen Anne.

POYNING'S LAW

Henry VII was very good at answering the Irish Question, and made a Law called Poyning's Law by which the Irish could have a Parliament of their own, but the English were to pass all the Acts in it. This was obviously a very Good Thing.

AGE OF DARING DISCOVERIES

The reign of Henry VII marks the end of the Middle Ages. These were succeeded by an age of daring discoveries, such as when Caprornicus observed the Moon while searching the skies with a telescope, thus causing the rotation of the Earth, crops, etc. Emboldened by this, Caprornicus began openly discussing the topic of capricorns, for which he was unanimously put to death.

The greatest of these discoveries, however, was St Christophus Columba, the utterly memorable American, who, with the assistance of the intrepid adventurers John and Sebastian Robot, discovered how to make an egg stand on its wrong end. (Modern History is generally dated from this event.)

TEST PAPER III

UP TO THE END OF HENRY VII

1. Contract, Expand and Explode
   (*a*) The Charters and Garters of the Realm.
   (*b*) The Old Suspender.
2. How did any *one* of the following differ from any one of the other?
   (1) Henry IV, Part I.
   (2) Henry IV, Part II.
3. 'The end of the closing of the 2nd stage of the Treaty of Bretigny marks the opening of a new phase in the 1st stage of the termination of the Hundred Years War.' (Confute.)
4. 'Know ye not Agincourt?' (Confess.)
5. 'Uneasy lies the head that wears a Throne.'
   (*a*) Suggest remedies, or
   (*b*) Imitate the action of a Tiger.
6. Intone interminably (but inaudibly)
   i   The Pilgrims' Grace.
   ii   'Cuccu.'
7. Do not draw a skotch-map of the Battle of Bannockburn, but write not more than three lines on the advantages and disadvantages of the inductive historical method with special relation to ecclesiastical litigation in the earlier Lancastrian epochs.
8. How would you confuse
   (1) The Wars of the Roses?
   (2) Lamnel Simkin and Percy Warmneck?
   (3) The Royal issue?
9. Why do you picture John of Gaunt as a rather emaciated grandee?
10. Describe in excessive detail
    (*a*) The advantages of the Black Death.
    (*b*) The fate of the Duke of Clarence.
    (*c*) A Surfeit.

N.B. – Candidates should write on at least one side of the paper.

IOHANNES FILIVS QVARTV
EDVARDI TERTII REX
CASTELLA ET LEGIONE
DVX LANCASTELIÆ
CONSTABVLARIVS CASTR
DE QVEENSBOVG COVIN
TO OCTOBRIS ANNO
REGNI EDW TERT ANN
GLIA 50 FRANCIA 37

'A rather emaciated grandee'

CHAPTER XXXI

BLUFF KING HAL

HENRY VIII was a strong King with a very strong sense of humour and VIII wives, memorable amongst whom were Katherine the Arrogant, Anne of Cloves, Lady Jane Austin and Anne Hathaway. His beard was, however, red.

In his youth Henry was fond of playing tennis and after his accession is believed never to have lost a set. He also invented a game called '*Bluff King Hal*' which he invited his ministers to play with him. The players were blindfolded and knelt down with their heads on a block of wood; they then guessed whom the King would marry next.

Cardinal Wolsey, the memorable homespun statesman and inventor of the Wolsack, played this game with Henry and won. But his successor, Cromwell (*not to be confused with Cromwell*), after winning on points, was disqualified by the King (who always acted as umpire), and lost.

In the opinion of Shakespeare (the memorable playwriter and Top Poet) his unexpected defeat was due to his failure to fling away ambition.

THE RESTORATION

Henry wanted the Pope to give him a divorce from his first wife, Katherine. He wanted this because

'*The memorable homespun statesman*'

'A strong King'

(a)   she was Arrogant.
(b)   he had married her a very long time ago.
(c)   when she had a baby it turned out to be Broody
Mary, and Henry wanted a boy.
(d)   he thought it would a Good Thing.

The Pope, however, refused, and seceded with all his
followers from the Church of England. This was called the
Restoration.

HENRY'S PLAN FAILS

Curiously enough Henry had all the time had an idea about a new wife for himself called Anne, who, he thought, looked as if she would be sure to have a son. So when the Divorce was all over (or nearly) he married her; but he was wrong about Anne, because she had a girl too, in a way (see Elizabeth).

After this Henry was afraid his reign would not be long enough for any more divorces, so he gave them up and executed his wives instead.* He also got less interested in his wives and gave himself up to Diplomacy, spending a great deal of his time playing tennis, etc., with the young King of France in a field called the Field of the Crock of Gold.

'Married her a long time ago'

END OF WOLSEY

Cardinal Wolsey, although (as is well known) he had not thought to shed a tear about all this, did ultimately shed a memorable one. Having thus fallen from grace (indeed he had already been discovered entertaining some Papal Bulls) Wolsey determined to make a Pilgrimage to Leicester Abbey, saying to himself: 'If I had served my God as I have served my King, I would have been a Good Thing.' Having thus acknowledged that he was a Bad Man, and being in due course arrived at the Abbey, Wolsey very pluckily expired after making a memorable speech to the Prior, beginning, 'Father Abbot, I come to lay my bones among you, Not to praise them . . .'

THE MONASTERIES

One of the strongest things that Henry VIII did was about the Monasteries. It was pointed out to him that no one in

---

* NOTE. – All except Anne of Cloves, whom he had on approval from Belgium and sent back on discovering that she was really not a queen at all but a 'fat mare with glanders'.

the monasteries was married, as the Monks all thought it was still the Middle Ages. So Henry, who, of course, considered marrying a Good Thing, told Cromwell to pass a very strong Act saying that the Middle Ages were all over and the monasteries were all to be dissolved. This was called the Disillusion of the Monasteries.

CHAPTER XXXII

EDWARD VI AND BROODY MARY

EDWARD VI and Broody Mary were the two small Tudors who came in between the two big ones, Henry VIII and Elizabeth. Edward VI was only a boy and consequently was not allowed to have his reign properly, but while he was sitting on the throne everyone in the land was forced to become Protestant, so that Broody Mary would be able to put them to death afterwards for not being Roman Catholics. A good many people protested against this treatment and thus it was proved that they were Protestants, but most of the people decanted and were all right. Broody Mary's reign was, however, a Bad Thing, since England is bound to be C of E, so all the executions were wasted.

CRAMBER AND FATIMER

It was about this time that a memorable Dumb Crammer and one of Henry VIII's wives called Fatimer, who had survived him, got burnt alive at Oxford, while trying to light a candle in the Martyr's memorial there: it was a new candle which they had invented and which they said could never be put out.

Shortly after this the cruel Queen died and a post-mortem examination revealed the word 'CALLOUS' engraved on her heart.

'Her heart'

'The two small Tudors'

CHAPTER XXXIII

ELIZABETH

ALTHOUGH this memorable Queen was a man, she was constantly addressed by her courtiers by various affectionate female nicknames, such as Aurora-borealis, Ruritania, Black Beauty (or Bête Noire) and Brown Bess. She also very graciously walked on Sir Walter Raleigh's overcoat whenever he dropped it in the mud and was, in fact, in every respect a good and romantic Queen.

'Aurora Borealis'

WAVE OF BEARDS

One of the most romantic aspects of the Elizabethan age was the wave of beards which suddenly swept across History and settled upon all the great men of the period. The most memorable of these beards was the cause of the outstanding event of the reign, which occurred in the following way.

'Wave of Beards'

'Spanish Mane'

THE GREAT ARMADILLO

The Spaniards complained that Captain F. Drake, the memorable bowlsman, had singed the King of Spain's beard (or Spanish Mane, as it was called) one day when it was in Cadiz Harbour. Drake replied that he was in his hammock at the time and a thousand miles away. The King of Spain, however, insisted that the beard had been spoilt and sent the Great Spanish Armadillo to ravish the shores of England.

The crisis was badly faced in England, especially by Big Bess herself, who instantly put on an enormous quantity of clothing and rode to and fro on a white horse at Tilbury – a courageous act which was warmly applauded by the English sailors.

In this striking and romantic manner the English were once more victorious.

'The memorable bowlsman'

'The Great Spanish Armadillo'

THE QUEEN OF HEARTS

A great nuisance in this reign was the memorable Scottish queen, known as Mary Queen of Hearts on account of the large number of husbands which she obtained, e.g. Cardinale Ritzio, Boswell and the King of France: most of these she easily blew up at Holywood.

Unfortunately for Mary, Scotland was now suddenly overrun by a wave of Synods led by Sir John Nox, the memorable Scottish Saturday Knight. Unable to believe, on account of the number of her husbands, that Mary was a single person, the Knight accused her of being a 'monstrous regiment of women', and after making this brave remark had her imprisoned in Loch Lomond. Mary, however, escaped and fled to England, where Elizabeth immediately put her in quarantine on the top of an enormous Height called Wutheringay.

As Mary had already been Queen of France and Queen of Scotland many people thought that it would be unfair if she was not made Queen of England as well. Various plots, such as the Paddington Plot, the Threadneedle Conspiracy and the Adelfi Plot, were therefore hatched to bring this about.

'Too romantic not to be executed'

Elizabeth, however, learning that in addition to all this Mary was good-looking and could play on the virginals, recognized that Mary was too romantic not to be executed, and accordingly had that done.

MASSACRE OF ST BARTHOLOMEW

Further evidence of Queen Elizabeth's chivalrous nature is given by her sympathy towards the French Protestants or Hugonauts (so called on account of their romantic leader Victor Hugo). These Arguenots were very much incensed at this time about St Bartholomew, a young Saint, who had been unjustly massacred for refusing to tie a white hand-kerchief round his arm. After the massacre the French King, Henry of Navarre, turned Roman Catholic and made his memorable confession – 'Paris is rather a Mess'; where-upon Queen Elizabeth very gallantly sent her favourite, Leicester, to find out whether this was true, thus rendering valuable assistance to the Hugonot cause.

ELIZABETH AND ESSEX

Memorable amongst the men with beards in Elizabeth's reign was the above-mentioned favourite, Essex (Robert Dudleigh, Earl of Leicester), whom she brought to ex-ecution by mistake in the following romantic manner. Essex was sent to Ireland to quell a rebellion which the Irish were very treacherously carrying on in a bog in Munster. Becom-ing fatigued with the rebellion, however, he dashed out of the bog straight into the Queen's bedroom. For this Essex was sent to the Tower, where he was shortly afterwards joined by other favourites of the Queen (such as Burleigh, Sidneigh, Watneigh, Hurlingham, etc.). Essex had a secret arrangement with Queen Elizabeth that he was to give her a ring whenever he was going to be executed, and she would reprieve him. But although, according to the arrangement, he tried to get into communication with the Queen, he was

given the wrong number and was thus executed after all, along with the other favourites.

'God may forgive you,' was Brown Bess's memorable comment to the operator, 'but I never will.'

CHAPTER XXXIV

JAMES I, A TIDY KING

JAMES I slobbered at the mouth and had favourites; he was thus a Bad King. He had, however, a very logical and tidy mind, and one of the first things he did was to have Sir Walter Raleigh executed for being left over from the previous reign. He also tried to straighten out the memorable confusion about the Picts, who, as will be remembered, were originally Irish living in Scotland, and the Scots, originally Picts living in Ireland. James tried to make things tidier by putting the Scots in Ulsters and

'Planting them in Ireland'

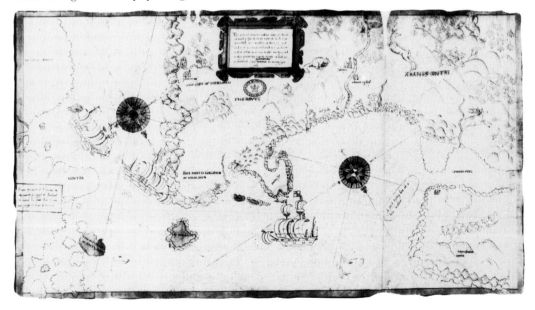

planting them in Ireland, but the plan failed because the Picts had been lost sight of during the Dark Ages and were now nowhere to be found.

GUNPOWDER PLOT

There were a great many plots and Parliaments in James I's reign, and one of the Parliaments was called the Addled

'A very loyal plan'

Parliament because the plots hatched in it were all such rotten ones. One plot, however, was by far the best plot in History, and the day and month of it (though not, of course, the year) are well known to be *utterly* and even maddeningly MEMORABLE.

The Gunpowder Plot arose in the following way: the King had recently invented a new table called *Avoirduroi*, which said:

I New Presbyter = I OLD PRIEST
0 Bishop   = 0 King

James was always repeating, 'No Bishop, No King,' to himself, and one day a certain loyal citizen called Sir Guyfawkes, a very active and conscientious man, overheard him, and thought it was the slogan of James's new policy. So he decided to carry it out at once and made a very loyal plan to blow up the King and the bishops and everybody else in Parliament assembled, with gunpowder.* Although the plan failed attempts are made every year on St Guyfawkes' Day to remind the Parliament that it would have been a *Good Thing*.

PILGRIMS' PROGRESS

It was at this time that some very pious Englishmen, known as the Early Fathers, who were being persecuted for not learning *Avoirduroi*, sailed away to America in a ship called the *Mayfly*; this is generally referred to as the Pilgrims' Progress and was one of the chief causes of America.

CHAPTER XXXV

CHARLES I AND THE CIVIL WAR

W ITH the ascension of Charles I to the throne we come at last to the Central Period of English History (not to be confused with the Middle

'Under these circumstances'

* Recently invented by Francis Bacon, author of Shakespeare, etc.

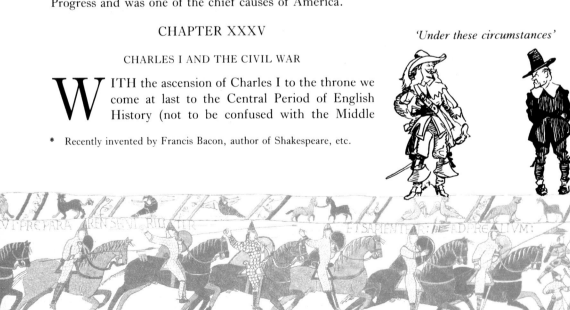

'A small pointed beard, long flowing curls'

Ages, of course), consisting in the *utterly memorable Struggle between the Cavaliers (Wrong but Wromantic) and the Roundheads (Right but Repulsive)*.

Charles I was a Cavalier King and therefore had a small pointed beard, long flowing curls, a large, flat, flowing hat and *gay attire*. The Roundheads, on the other hand, were clean-shaven and wore tall, conical hats, white ties and *sombre garments*. Under these circumstances a Civil War was inevitable.

The Roundheads, of course, were so called because Cromwell had all their heads made perfectly round, in order that they should present a uniform appearance when drawn up in line.

Besides this, if any man lost his head in action, it could be used as a cannon-ball by the artillery (which was done at the Siege of Worcester).

COMPETITION OF RIGHT

For a long time before the Civil War, however, Charles had been quarrelling with the Roundheads about what was right. Charles explained that there was a doctrine called the Divine Right of Kings, which said that:

(*a*) He was King, and that was right.
(*b*) Kings were divine, and that was right.

'The Divine Right of Kings'

(c) Kings were right, and that was right.

(d) Everything was all right.

But so determined were the Roundheads that all this was all wrong that they drew up a Petition called the Petition of Right to show in more detail which things were wrong. This Petition said:

(a) That it was wrong for anyone to be put to death more than once for the same offence.

(b) *Habeas Corpus*, which meant that it was wrong if people were put in prison except for some reason, and that people who had been mutilated by the King, such as Prynne, who had often had his ears cut off, should always be allowed to keep their bodies.

(c) That Charles's memorable methods of getting money, such as Rummage and Scroungeage, were wrong.

But the most important cause of the Civil War was

SHIP MONEY

Charles I said that any money which was Ship Money belonged to him; but while the Roundheads declared that Ship Money could be found only in the Cinq Ports, Charles maintained that no one but the King could guess right which was Ship Money and which wasn't. This was, of course, part of his Divine Right. The climax came when a villager called Hampden (memorable for his dauntless breast) advised the King to divine again.

This so upset Charles that he went back to Westminster, and after cinquing several ports burst into the House of Commons and asked in a very royal way for some birds which he said were in there. The Parliament, who were mostly Puritans, were so shocked that they began making

solemn Leagues and Countenances. Charles therefore became very angry and complaining that the birds had flown raised his standard at Nottingham and declared war against Hampden and the Roundheads.

THE WAR

At first the King was successful owing to Prince Rupert of Hentzau, his famous cavalry leader, who was very dashing in all directions. After this, many indecisive battles were fought at such places as Newbury, Edgehill, Sedgehill, Newbury, Chalgrove Field, Newbury, etc., in all of which the Cavaliers were rather victorious.

The Roundheads therefore made a new plan in order to win the war after all. This was called the Self-Denying Ordnance and said that everyone had to deny everything he had done up to that date, and that nobody was allowed to admit who he was: thus the war could be started again from the beginning. When the Roundheads had done this they were called the New Moral Army and were dressed up as Ironclads and put under the command of Oliver Cromwell, whose Christian name was Oliver and who was therefore affectionately known as 'Old Nick'. Cromwell was not only moral and completely round in the head but had a large (round) wart on the nose. He was consequently victorious in all the remaining battles such as Newbury, Marston Moor, Edgehill (change for Chalgrove), Naseby, Newbury, etc.

BLOOD AND IRONCLADS

When Charles I had been defeated he was brought to trial by the Rump Parliament – so called because it had been sitting for such a long time – and was found guilty of being defeated in a war against himself, which was, of course, a form of High Treason. He was therefore ordered by Cromwell to go and have his head cut off (it was, the Roundheads pointed out, the wrong shape, anyway). So

'Very memorable'

'A large round wart'

romantic was Charles, however, that this made little difference to him and it is very memorable that he walked and talked Half an hour after his Head was cut off.

On seeing this Cromwell was so angry that he picked up the mace (the new and terrible Instrument of Government which he had invented) and, pointing it at the Head, shouted: 'Take away that Marble,' and announced that his policy in future would be just Blood and Ironclads. In order to carry out this policy he divided the country into twelve districts and set a Serjeant-Major over each of them.

RULE OF THE SERJEANT-MAJOR

Nothing sickened the people of the rule of the Serjeant-Major so much as their cruel habit of examining little boys *viva-voce*. For this purpose the unfortunate children were dressed in their most uncomfortable satins and placed on a

stool. The Serjeant-Major would then ask such difficult questions as 'How's your Father?' or 'Animal, Vegetable or Mineral?' and those who could not answer were given a cruel medicine called Pride's Purge. All this was called the · Commonwealth and was right but repulsive.

THE CROWNING MERCY

The Roundheads at length decided to offer Cromwell the Crown. Cromwell, however, was unwilling and declared it was a Crowning Mercy when he found that it would not fit, having been designed for a Cavalier King.

Soon after Cromwell died of a surfeit of Pride, Purges, Warts and other Baubles.

CHAPTER XXXVI

CHARLES II, A MERRY MONARCH

C HARLES II was always very merry and was therefore not so much a king as a Monarch. During the civil war he had rendered valuable assistance to his father's side by hiding in all the oak trees he could find. He was thus very romantic and popular and was able after the death of Cromwell to descend to the throne.

Though now no longer arboreal, Charles remained very much interested in natural beauty and kept a great number of pets at his court, including his famous *King Charles's Spaniards*, the most memorable of whom was Catherine of Braganza; but, although married to Catherine, Charles was even fonder of an orange girl called Elinor Gwyn. He was thus a Bad Man.

'A Bad Man'

'Very interested in natural beauty'

THE REFORMATION

Charles II was famous for his wit and his inventions. Among the latter was an unbridled and merry way of behaving and writing plays, called the Reformation. This was a Good Thing in the end as it was one of the earliest causes of Queen Victoria's determination to be good.

EXAMPLES OF CHARLES'S WIT

Most of Charles's witty remarks were of an *unbridled nature* and therefore (unfortunately) *not memorable*.

He instituted however a number of witty Acts of Parliament. Amongst these were:

(a) The *Act of Indemnity and Oblivion*, which said that everyone had to pay an indemnity to the King and then forget that he had paid it.

(b) The *Act of Uniformity*, which said that everyone had to be the same as everyone else.

(c) The *Five Mile Act*, which said that no schoolmasters or clergymen were to go within five miles of each other. (This was, obviously, a Good Thing.).

(d) The *Corporation Act*, which said that everyone had to be as fat as possible (except Nell Glyn.)

After each of these Charles became merrier still and though some of them, particularly the Corporation Act, were considered rather unfair, he made up by passing a new Habeas Corpus Act which said that *all* the people might keep their bodies, and thus everyone was contented. Later, Charles became even merrier and made a *Declaration of Indulgence* saying that people could do anything they liked and a *Test Act* was passed soon after to see if they had done it (and, if so, what).

ADMIRAL DE TROP IN THE CHANNEL (REUTER)

It was at this period that the Navigation Acts were first

'It caused some wars against the Dutch'

made by the English. These Acts pointed out to the other countries that no foreign ships knew how to navigate the seas, and that their only chance was to steer for English ports. Although this was really part of the Rule Britannia (see Chap. II, Freedom of the Seas), it caused some wars against the Dutch who were treacherously attempting to be top nation on the sea at that time. For a short while the Dutch ships were successful under their memorable Admiral, Van Broom, who is famous for blowing his own Trompet up the Medway until the sound was heard in the

streets of London. The war, however, soon came to an end, since the Dutch are quite small and can never be top nation really.

QUAKER OATES

A great deal of excitement was caused in this reign by Titus Oates, the memorable Quaker, who said that a Roman Catholic plot had been made with the objects

- (*a*)   of murdering the King
- (*b*)   of blowing up the people
- (*c*)   of restoring the Roman Catholic religion instead.

These would probably have been a Bad Thing, if they had been achieved, and the King was so enraged that he immediately introduced a *Disabling Act* which said that everyone except the heir to the throne was to be disabled. Later when he had relented, he had another *Habeas Corpus Act* passed, saying that the disabled people might keep their bodies.

TWO GOOD THINGS

During Charles II's reign the Great Plague happened in London. This was caused by some rats which had left a sinking ship on its way from China, and was very fortunate for the Londoners, since there were too many people in London at the time, so that they were always in bad health.

In the following year, therefore, London was set on fire in case anyone should have been left over from the Plague, and St Paul's Cathedral was built instead. This was also a Good Thing and was the cause of Sir Christopher Wren, the memorable architect.

PEPYS

Among the famous characters of the period were Samuel Pepys, who is memorable for keeping a Dairy and going to

'London was set on fire'

bed a great deal, and his wife Evelyn, who kept another memorable Dairy, but did not go to bed in it.

CHAPTER XXXVII

JAMES II, A MADDENING KING

ALTHOUGH a Good Man, James II was a Bad King and behaved in such an irritating and arbitrary way that by the end of his reign the people had all gone mad.

JUDGE JEFFREYS

One of the first things that happened was a rebellion by Monmouth, an indiscriminate son of Charles II who, landing incorrectly in Somerset, was easily defeated at

'Pepys' wife, Evelyn'

Newbury, Sedgehill, Marston Moor, Newbury, etc. (see Civil War). The Rebels were ferociously dealt with by the memorable Judge Jeffreys who was sent out by James as a Justice in Ire in the West, where he made some furious remarks about the prisoners, known as 'The Bloody Asides'.

MADNESSES OF JAMES II

James II further enraged his subjects by

(*a*) attempting to repeal the Habeas Corpus Act, saying that nobody might have a body after all, and

(*b*) claiming the Dispensing Power which was a threat to revive Pride's Purge and do the dispensing of it himself;

(*c*) suspending (probably a modified form of hanging) the Vice-Chancellor at Cambridge, who was apparently mad too, for refusing to have a Benedictine.

'Bloody Asides'

ENGLAND'S ANSWER

The final and irreparable madness of the people was brought on by James's action in bringing to trial Seven Bishops (Bancroft, Sancroft and Sacheveral others) for refusing to read Charles II's Declaration of Indulgence (which they thought would be dangerous under the circumstances), and when in addition it became known that James had confined his infant son and heir in a warming-pan the people lost control of themselves altogether and, lighting an enormous number of candles, declared that *the answer was an Orange*. James was thus compelled to abdicate.

CHAPTER XXXVIII

WILLIAMANMARY, ENGLAND RULED BY AN ORANGE

W ILLIAMANMARY for some reason was known as The Orange in their own country of Holland, and were popular as King of England because

the people naturally believed it was descended from Nell Glyn. It was on the whole a good King and one of their first Acts was the Toleration Act, which said they would tolerate anything, though afterwards it went back on this and decided that they could not tolerate the Scots.

'The Answer'

A DARIEN SCHEME

The Scots were now in a skirling uproar because James II was the last of the Scottish Kings and England was under the rule of the Dutch Orange; it was therefore decided to put them in charge of a very fat man called Cortez and transport them to a Peak in Darien, where it was hoped they would be more silent.

MASSACRE OF GLASCOE

The Scots, however, continued to squirl and hoot at the Orange, and a rebellion was raised by the memorable Viscount Slaughterhouse (the Bonnie Dundee) and his Gallivanting Army. Finally Slaughterhouse was defeated at the Pass of Ghilliekrankie and the Scots were all massacred at Glascoe, near Edinburgh (in Scotland, where the Scots were living at that time); after which they were forbidden to curl or hoot or even to wear the Kilt. (This was a Good Thing, as the Kilt was one of the causes of their being so uproarious and Scotch.)

BLOOD-ORANGEMEN

Meanwhile the Orange increased its popularity and showed themselves to be a very strong King by its ingenious answer to the Irish Question; this consisted in the Battle of the Boyne and a very strong treaty which followed it, stating

(*a*) that all the Irish Roman Catholics who liked could be transported to France.

(*b*) that all the rest who liked could be put to the sword.

(*c*) that Northern Ireland should be planted with Blood-Orangemen.

These Blood-Orangemen are still there; they are, of course, all descendants of Nell Glyn and are extremely fierce and industrial and so loyal that they are always ready to start a loyal rebellion to the Glory of God and the Orange. All of which shows that the Orange was a Good Thing, as well as being a good King.

After the Treaty the Irish who remained were made to go and live in a bog and think of a New Question.

'Memorable dead queen, Anne'

THE BANK OF ENGLAND

It was Williamanmary who first discovered the National
Debt and had the memorable idea of building the Bank of
England to put it in. The National Debt is a very Good
Thing and it would be dangerous to pay it off, for fear of
Political Economy.

Finally the Orange was killed by a mole while out riding
and was succeeded by the memorable dead queen, Anne.

TEST PAPER IV

UP TO THE END OF THE STUARTS

1. Stigmatise cursorily (*a*) Queen Mary, (*b*) Judge Jeffreys's asides. (Speak out.)
2. Outline joyfully (1) Henry VIII, (2) Stout Cortez.
3. Who had what written on whose what?
4A. What convinces you that Henry VIII had VIII wives? Was it worth it?
4B. Conjugate briefly Ritzio and Mary Queen of Scots.
5. In what ways was Queen Elizabeth a Bad Man but a Good Queen?
6. 'To the exercise of Despotic Monarchy the Crown is more essential than the Throne.' (Refute with special reference to anything you know.)
7A. Which do you consider was the strongest swimmer, (*a*) The Spanish Armadillo, (*b*) The Great Seal?
7B. Who was in whose what, and how many miles awhat?
7C. Cap'n, art thou sleeping there below?*
8. Deplore the failure of the Gunpowder Plot, stating the day and month (but not, of course, the year) usually assigned to it.
9. Examine the state of mind of
   (1) Charles I, half an hour after his head was cut off.
   (2) Charles II, half a moment after first sighting Nell Gwyn.
10. Why on earth was William of Orange? (Seriously, though.)
11. How can you be so numb and vague about Arabella Stuart?
12. Estimate the medical prowess of the period with clinical reference to (*a*) Pride's Purge, (*b*) The Diet of Worms, (*c*) The Topic of Capricorns.

* N.B. – Do not attempt to answer this question.

CHAPTER XXXIX

ANNE, A DEAD QUEEN

QUEEN ANNE was considered rather a remarkable woman and hence was usually referred to as Great Anna, or Annus Mirabilis. Besides being dead she was extremely kind-hearted and had a very soothing Act passed called the *Occasional Conformity Act* which said that people only had to conform with it occasionally: this pleasant trait in her character was called Queen Anne's Bounty. (The Occasional Conformity Act was the only Act of its kind in History, until the Speed limit was invented.)

The Queen had many favourites (all women), the most memorable of whom were Sarah Jenkins and Mrs Smashems, who were the first Wig and the first Tory. Sarah Jenkins was really the wife of the Duke of Marlborough, the famous General, inventor of the Ramillies Whig, of which Sarah wore the first example.

SUCCESSION OF WARS

All through the XVIIIth Century there was a Succession of Wars, and in Queen Anne's reign these were called the Spanish Succession (or Austrian Succession) because of The Infanta (or The Maria-theresa); they were fought mainly on account of the French King L/XIV (le grand Monomarque) saying there were *no more Pyrenese*, thus infuriating the Infanta who was one herself.

Probably the Wars could never have been fought properly but for the genius of Marlborough, who could always remember which side the Bavarians and the Elector Pantomime of the Rhine were supposed to be on: this unique talent enabled him to defeat his enemies in fierce battles long before they could discover which side he himself was on. Marlborough, however, was a miser in politics and made everyone pay to go into his party; he was therefore despised as a *turnstyle*.

In this reign also occurred the memorable Port Wine Treaty with Portugal, directed against Decanters (as the Non-Conformists were now called), as well as a very clever Act called the Schism Act which said that everybody's religion was to be quite different from everybody else's. Meanwhile the Whigs being the first to realise that the Queen had been dead all the time chose George I as King.

CHAPTER XL

THE XV AND THE XLV

'Late for his own Rebellion'

ALTHOUGH the Whigs said that George I was King, many of the Tories thought that the Old Pretender was. The Old Pretender did not raise the standard of rebellion much and is only famous for being late for his own Rebellion, which had been easily put down long before he landed with his memorable XV in Scotland. His standard was of blue silk with the motto '*Nemo me impune lacessit*', but when it was raised the top fell off.

The Young Pretender, whose followers were called the XLV, was quite different, his standard being of red silk with the motto '*Tandem Triumphans*', and the top didn't fall off. At Preston Pans the English commander was the first to run away and bring the news of his own defeat, which was thus immediately believed. The hero of these adventures was the memorable Bonnie Prince Charlie (the Young Chandelier), who after being bloodily defeated by a Butcher at Flodden in Cumberland, was helped to escape by his many Scottish lovers, such as Flora MacNightingale (the fair maid of Perth), Amy Robsart, Lorna Doone, Annie Laurie, the Widow with Thumbs, etc.

THE SOUTHSEA BUBBLE

About this time nearly everybody in London stupidly got involved in an enormous bubble that appeared at Southsea. Some were persuaded that it would be a Good Thing if all

the money in the country, including the National Debt, were sunk in it; others got into it merely with the object of speculating how soon it would be before it burst. Among these was a very clever man called Walpole who got out of the bubble in time, thus bursting it and becoming the first Prime Minister. Walpole was a Good Prime Minister; the Southsea bubble was thus a Good Thing.

'LET SLEEPING DOGS LIE' (WALPOLE)

Walpole ought never to be confused with Walpole, who was quite different; it was Walpole who lived in a house with the unusual name of Strawberry Jam and spent his time writing letters to famous men (such as the Prime Minister, Walpole, etc.). Walpole is memorable for inventing the new policy of letting dogs go to sleep. This was a Good Thing really, but it so enraged the people (who thought that a dog's life should be more uncomfortable) that they rang all the bells in London. At first Walpole merely muttered his policy, but eventually he was compelled to rouse himself and become actively memorable by remarking: 'They are ringing the bells now; I shall be wringing their necks soon.'

'Walpole lived in a house with the unusual name of Strawberry Jam'

CHAPTER XLI

RULES OF WARS IN THE XVIIITH CENTURY

ALTHOUGH the Succession of Wars went on nearly the whole time in the XVIIIth Century, the countries kept on making a treaty called the Treaty of Paris (or Utrecht).

This Treaty was a Good Thing and laid down the Rules for fighting the wars; these were:

(1) that there should be a mutual restitution of conquests except that England should keep Gibraltar, Malta, Minorca, Canada, India, etc.;

(2) that France should hand over to England the West

'Policy'

'An enormous bubble at Southsea'

Indian islands of San Flamingo, Tapioca, Sago, Dago, Bezique and Contango, while the Dutch were always to have Lumbago and the Laxative Islands;

(3) that everyone, however Infantile or even insane, should renounce all claim to the Spanish throne;

(4) that the King (or Queen) of France should admit that the King (or Queen) of England was King (or Queen) of England and should not harbour the Young Pretender, but that *the fortifications of Dunkirk should be disgruntled and raised to the ground.*

Thus, as soon as the fortifications of Dunkirk had been

gruntled again, or the Young Pretender was found in a harbour in France, or it was discovered that the Dutch had not got Lumbago, etc., the countries knew that it was time for the treaty to be signed again, so that the War could continue in an orderly manner.

CHAPTER XLII

GEORGE III, AN OBSTINATE KING

G EORGE III was a Bad King. He was, however, to a great extent insane and a Good Man and his ministers were always called Pitt. The Pitts, like Pretenders, generally came in waves of about two, an elder Pitt and a younger Pitt.

'Wave of Pitts'

BRITAIN MUFFLES THROUGH

The elder Pitt (Clapham) at this time had the rather strategic idea of conquering Canada on the banks of the Elbe; learning, however, that it was not there he told the famous poetic general, Wolfe, to conquer Quebec instead. At first Wolfe complained that he would rather write Gray's Elegy, but on being told that it had been written already (by Gray) he agreed to take Quebec.

Quebec was very difficult to approach; Wolfe therefore rowed up the St Laurence with muffled drums and ordered his Highland troops to skirl up the perpendicular Heights of Abraham with muffled boots, hoots, etc, thus taking the French by surprise.

At this engagement the French had a very peculiar general with the unusual French name of Keep-calm.

On receiving a muffled report to the effect that Wolfe's men had captured Quebec, one of his aides-de-calm called out: 'See! They fly!' 'Who fly?' asked the General, and, on being assured that it was his own men who were flying, 'Thank God!' said Keep-calm, with a sigh of satisfaction: 'Now, I can fly in peace!'

'Britain muffles through'

'A Bad King'

CHAPTER XLIII

INDIA

I T was in the 18th Century that Indian History
started. Indian History is a great number of wars in
which the English fought victoriously against the
Waratah Confederacy and various kinds of potentates called

Sahibs, Wallahs, Jahs, Rajahs, Hurrahjahs, Mahurrahjahs, Jhams, and Jhelhies. Most memorable amongst these were the terrible Napoo Sahib, the Maharatta of Pshaw, the Chandra Gaff and the Taj Mahal.

CRESSEY AND THE BLACK WHOLE

Many of these victories were due to an Englishman named Robert Clive, a typist in the East India Coy Ltd, who, after failing to commit suicide three times, made the famous raid on Arcos in conjunction with Jicks Pasha, and held it against all corners.

Clive then marched to Calcutta and with a Mir Jafar (or handful) of men defeated all the Indians in the utterly memorable battle of Cressey.

This battle was Clive's revenge on the Black Whole of Calcutta and especially on that destructive All-Black Waratah, the Napoo Sahib.

THE DOLDRUMS OF OUDH

Second in importance only to Clive was Laurence Hastings, well known for his rapacity towards the natives. Besides his treatment of Lo (a poor Indian with an untutored mind), recorded by the poet Poep, he very harshly extracted money from the Doldrums of Oudh, two old women without any teeth. For this he was impaled before the House of Commons, and after being cross-examined by Burke and Hare for seven and a half years, was finally acquitted and became Viscount Senlac of Oudh.

CHAPTER XLIV

THE BOSTON TEA-PARTY

ONE day when George III was insane he heard that the Americans never had afternoon tea. This made him very obstinate and he invited them all to a

compulsory tea-party at Boston; the Americans, however, started by pouring the tea into Boston Harbour and went on pouring things into Boston Harbour until they were quite Independent, thus causing the United States. These were also partly caused by Dick Washington who defeated the English at Bunker's Hill ('with his little mashie', as he told his father afterwards).

The War with the Americans is memorable as being the only war in which the English were ever defeated, and it was unfair because the Americans had *the Allies* on their side. In some ways the war was really a draw, since England remained top nation and had the Allies afterwards, while the Americans, in memory of George III's madness, still refuse to drink tea and go on pouring anything the English send them to drink into Boston Harbour.

After this the Americans made Wittington President and gave up speaking English and became U.S.A. and Columbia and 100%, etc. This was a Good Thing in the end, as it was the cause of the British Empire, but it prevented America from having any more History.

'100%, etc.'

CHAPTER XLV

THE FRENCH REVOLUTION

SOON after America had ceased to be memorable, the French Revolution broke out (in France). This, like all other Revolutions, was chiefly due to Liberty, Fraternity, Equality, etc., but also to the writings of Madame Tousseau, the French King's mistress, who believed in everyone returning to a state of nature and was therefore known as *la belle sauvage*.

The French Revolution is very interesting and romantic; quite near the beginning of it Dante and Robespear, the revolutionary leaders (or *Jacobites* as they were called), met in the beautiful and historic Chamber of Horrors at Versailles and decided to massacre everyone in September.

'Liberty, Fraternity, Equality'

This was called the *Glorious First of June* and was done in accordance with a new *National Convention*. Memorable amongst those who were massacred were Robespear himself, who was executed in his own gelatine, and Marat, who was murdered in his bath by Madame Tousseau.

CHAPTER XLVI

NAPOLEON

THE English were disgusted by this new French Convention and so decided to go in for The War again, thus causing Napoleon and the Duke of Wellington. The War was now called the Napoleonic War, after Napoleon, a Corsican, whose real name was Bonuapart, who had cleverly made himself First Consort by means of a *whiff of grape-nuts*. (This is called the Napoleonic Legend.)

The French Revolution caused great loss of life, liberty, fraternity, etc., and was, of course, a Good Thing, since the French were rather degenerate at the time; but Napoleon now invented a new Convention that the French should massacre all the other nations and become top nation, and this, though quite generate, was a Bad Thing.

CHAPTER XLVII

NELSON

NAPOLEON ought never to be confused with Nelson, in spite of their hats being so alike; they can most easily be distinguished from one another by the fact that Nelson always stood with his arm *like this*, while Napoleon always stood with his arms *like that*.

Nelson was one of England's most naval officers, and despised weak commands. At one battle when he was told that his Admiral-in-Chief had ordered him to cease fire, he

'Nelson always stood with his arm like this'

put the telephone under his blind arm and exclaimed in disgust: 'Kiss me, Hardy!'

By this and other intrepid manoeuvres the French were utterly driven from the seas.

PITT AND FOX

Meanwhile at home the War was being helped on a good deal by the famous remarks of the politicians, such as Pitt and Fox. On one occasion Fox said in the House of Commons that the French Revolution was a Good Thing; whereupon the younger Pitt (Balham) rose slowly to his feet and, pointing at Fox, exclaimed: 'Roll up that chap: he will not be wanted these ten years.' Having thus made this most memorable saying, Pitt was carried out of the House and died almost immediately of a surfeit of austerlitz. The plans of Napoleon were thus gradually thwarted.

CHAPTER XLVIII

WELLINGTON

BUT the most important of the great men who at this time kept Britain top nation was an Irishman called John Wesley, who afterwards became the Duke of Wellington (and thus English). When he was still Wolseley, Wellington made a great name for himself at Plassaye, in India, where he

Fought with his fiery few and one

remarking afterwards, 'It was the bloodiest battle for numbers I ever knew.' It was, however, against Napoleon and his famous Marshals (such as Marshals Ney, Soult, Davos, Mürren, Soult, Blériot, Snelgrove, Ney, etc.) that Wellington became most memorable. Napoleon's armies

'To march on their Stomachs'

'Wellington'

always used to march on their stomachs, shouting: 'Vive l'Intérieur!' and so moved about very slowly (*ventre-à-terre*, as the French say) thus enabling Wellington to catch them up and defeat them. When Napoleon made his troops march all the way to Moscow on their stomachs they got frozen to death one by one, and even Napoleon himself admitted afterwards that it was rather a Bad Thing.

GORILLA WAR IN SPAIN

The second part of the Napoleonic War was fought in Spain and Portugal and was called the Gorilla War on account of the primitive Spanish method of fighting. Wellington became so impatient with the slow movements of the French troops that he occupied himself drawing imaginary lines all over Portugal and thus marking off the fighting zone; he made a rule that defeats beyond these lines did not

'Gorilla Warfare'

count, while any French army that came his side of them
was out of bounds. Having thus insured himself against
disaster, Wellington won startling victories at Devalera,
Albumina, Salamanda, etc.

WATERLOO

After losing this war Napoleon was sent away by the
French, since he had not succeeded in making them top
nation; but he soon escaped and returned just in time to
fight on the French side at the battle of Waterloo. This
utterly memorable battle was fought at the end of a dance,
on the Playing Fields of Eton, and resulted in the English
definitely becoming top nation. It was thus a very Good
Thing. During the engagement the French came on in their
usual creeping and crawling method and were defeated by

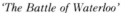

'The Battle of Waterloo'

'Napoleon stood on the deck in white breeches'

Wellington's memorable order, 'Up Jenkins and Smashems.'

This time Napoleon was sent right away for ever by everybody, and stood on the deck of a ship in white breeches and his arms *like that*.

CHAPTER XLIX

THE INDUSTRIAL REVELATION

D URING these Wars many very remarkable discoveries and inventions were made. Most memorable among these was the discovery (made by all the rich men in England at once) that women and children could work for 25 hours a day in factories without many of them dying or becoming excessively deformed. This was known as the Industrial Revelation and completely changed the faces of the North of England.

THE TRACTARIAN MOVEMENT

The Industrial Revelation would never have ocurred but for the wave of a great mechanical Inventors, e.g. Arkwright, who invented the Spinning Jenny, or unmarried textile

'Railway trains'

working girl; subsequently, however, this kind of work was done by mules, the discovery of a man called Crompton. Other benefactors were Sir Isaak Watts who invented steam-kettles, Sir Robert Boyle who had them legalized,* and finally Robert Louis Stevenson, who put wheels on to them, thereby inventing Railway trains, steam-rollers and other tractarian engines.

FACTORY ACTS

The new situation created by the Industrial Revelation was boldly met by the statesmen of the day with a wave of Acts, such as Tory Acts, Factory Acts, Satisfactory Acts and

---

* Boyle's Law: ('Watts pots never boyle').

'Mr Arkwright's Invention'

Unsatisfactory Acts. The most soothing of these enacted that children under 5 years of age who worked all day in factories should have meals (at night). This was a Good Thing, as it enabled them to work much faster.

ENCLOSURES

At the same time there was an Agricultural Revelation which was caused by the invention of turnips and the discovery that Trespassers would be Prosecuted. This was a Good Thing too, because previously the Land had all been rather common, and it was called the Enclosure movement and was the origin of Keeping off the Grass. The movement culminated in the vast Royal Enclosure at Ascot which nobody is allowed on except His Majesty the King (and friend).

THE COMBINATIONS LAW

All this gave rise to considerable discontent, but it was not until the memorable Combinations Law was passed that the people were roused to fury. This unjust law said that Combinations (or Union suits) were legal, or (in some cases) illegal, both for employers and employees, and resulted in the

'Combinations Law'

BLANKESTER MASSACRE

Gradually the people had become so discontented with the Combinations Law that they had begun wearing Blankets, especially in the North of England; this was, of course, sedition, and resulted in a battle near Manchester, in which all the people in blankets were accidentally massacred.

The Government then very cleverly passed the famous Six Acts, all of which said that it was quite all right for people in blankets to be massacred. Since which the people in the North have ceased to be seditious, and even wear bowler hats for lunch, bathing, etc.

MUNROE DOCTRINE

Meanwhile in foreign affairs, Canning, the memorable foreign minister, started a new anti-English or Liberal policy by saying that he had 'called the New World into existence to upset the Balance of the Old'. This was known as the Munroe Doctrine and proves that it is wrong for anyone to have wars in North or South America (except the United States Marines).

CHAPTER L

GEORGE IV, A GENTLEMAN KING

DURING these disturbances George III had died and had been succeeded by his son, George IV, who was the Prince Regent and an Inventor and very Bad. George IV's most memorable invention was Gentlemen and he was the First Gentleman in Europe:

EXAMPLES OF GEORGE IV'S BADNESS AND GENTLEMANLINESS

1. He was very fat.
2. He was a friend of Beau Brocade, the memorable Dandy Dinmont or man-about-town of those days.
3. He was a member of White's and many other notorious Knight clubs.
4. He was hostile to his wife and attempted to give her pains by means of an Act of Parliament.

DEATH OF GEORGE IV

Besides gentlemen, George IV had invented Regent Street, the Regent Canal, etc., before he came to the throne, and afterwards he invented the Brighton Marine Aquarium. He was thus a Bad Thing. Finally, he died of a surfeit of Aquaria, Pavilia, Gentlemen, etc., probably at Brighton.

'He was hostile to his wife'

CHAPTER LI

WILLIAM IV, A SAILOR KING

THE marine tendency of George IV was inherited by his brother William IV, who was known as the Sailor King on account of his readiness to create any number of piers at moments of political crisis. Apart from this, however, William IV would not have succeeded in being memorable at all except for his awkward and uncalled-for irruption into the Georgian succession.

'Brighton marine Aquarium'

ROTTEN BURROWS

During this reign the Great Reform Bill was passed on account of the Rotten Burrows: this was because the Old Landlords said that new places like Manchester were rotten burrows and shouldn't have votes. A great deal of confusion was caused by these rotten burrows which were undermining the Constitution, but eventually Lord Grey invented the Great Reform Bill which laid down clearly who had votes and who hadn't.

REFORM BILL

This Bill had two important clauses, which said:

(1) that some of the Burrows were rotten and that the people who lived in them should not be allowed either to stand or to have seats.

(2) that 'householders leasesholders and copyholders who had £10 in the towns or freeholders who paid 40/– in the country for 10 years or leaseholders (in

the country) and copyholders for 21 years in the
towns (paying a rent of £50) should in some cases
(in the towns) have a vote (for 1 year) but in others
for 41 years (in the country) paying a leasehold or
copyhold of £10 should not'.

When this unforgettable Law was made known there was
great rejoicing and bonfires were lit all over the country.

LATER REFORM BILLS

Later in the century, other Reform Bills were passed, such
as Gladstone's Reform Bill which added householders (in
the country) for one year to freeholders and kettleholders
worth £10 a year, and gave a vote to anyone who lived in
lodgings (for 21 years) or spent £10 in the Post Office.
And there was also Disraeli's Reform Bill, which gave the
vote to any lodger who paid £10 and lodged in the same
lodgings for one year. This, however, was naturally
thought very rash and was quite rightly characterised by
the penetrating Lord Salisbury, in a brilliant phrase, as 'A
Sleep in the Dark'. The Reform Bills were a Good Thing
except for a few Old Landlords who were deprived of their
seats. Nowadays Flappers are allowed to vote and men
have to put up with this even if they live in the same
lodgings all their lives. This is a Bad Thing and is called
Manhold Suffrage.

CHAPTER LII

QUEEN VICTORIA, A GOOD QUEEN

O N the death of William IV, Queen Victoria,
though asleep at the time and thus in her night-
dress, showed great devotion to duty by immediately ascending the throne. In this bold act she was assisted
by Lord Melbourne and the Archbishop of Canterbury,
who were both properly dressed.

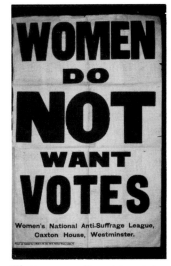

'Flappers are allowed to vote'

Finding herself on the throne, Queen Victoria immediately announced her intention of being Good and plural *but not amused*. This challenge was joyfully accepted by her subjects, and throughout her protracted reign *loyal and indefatigable attempts to amuse her* were made by Her Majesty's eminently Victorian ministers and generals.

'Good . . . but not amused'

ATTEMPTS TO AMUSE QUEEN VICTORIA

One of the first of these attempts was Lord Melbourne's memorable political rule that it did not matter what the Cabinet said so long as they all answered at once. This he called the Collective Responsibility of the Cabinet; the Queen, however, was not amused.

Next, Mr Rowland Hill invented penny stamps. The Queen, however, without hesitation Knighted him.

The loyal task therefore devolved on a more active group of men called the Chartists who nearly succeeded by drawing an enormous Chart showing the position of affairs and signing it with imaginary names. This resulted in a succession of riots amongst the imaginary people, and necessitated the passing of the memorable Poor Law which laid down that everybody in the country was poor (except the rich).

'To abandon all thoughts of levity –'

These endeavours having failed, the Queen was allowed to abandon for the time being all thoughts of levity and to marry her beautiful cousin (the memorable Prince Consaught), a Good German whom she had met during the great International Expedition to Hyde Park.

SIR ROBERT PEEL, POTATO DUTIES IN IRELAND

About this time the famous Tory statesman, Sir Robert Peel, noticed that the Irish had had nothing to eat for some years owing to the fact that the potatoes, which it was their Duty to eat, had all gone bad.

The Tory Government were for long divided between two policies, one section insisting that the Irish ought to eat the potatoes, the other insisting that they need not.

Sir Robert, however, boldly passed his famous Corn Laws which abolished the Duty and permitted the Irish to eat bread, thus dissociating himself from the Tories who doggedly maintained that the Irish had only two alternatives: (*a*) to eat the potatoes, and (*b*) not to. Sir Robert, having thus destroyed his own Party, bethought himself of The Queen and invented Policemen. Her Majesty, however . . .

CHAPTER LIII

CRIMEAN WAR

'Invented Policemen'

NOT very long after this the memorable Crimean War broke out against the Russians. This war was exceptionally inevitable and was caused by a number of causes.

CAUSES OF THE CRIMEAN WAR

(*a*) The English had not yet fought against the Russians.

(*b*) The *Sick Man of Europe* (cured later by Florence Nightingown).

(*c*) Russia was too big and was pointing in the direction of India.

(*d*) The *Holy Places. The French* thought that the *Holy Places* ought to be guarded (probably against the *Americans*) by *Latin Monks*, while *the Turks*, who owned the Places, thought that they ought to be guarded by *Greek Monks. England* therefore quite rightly declared war on *Russia*, who immediately occupied *Roumania*.

The war was consequently fought in *the Crimea* (near *Persia*) in the following romantic manner:

1. *The Battle of Inkerman* – so called because the

soldiers on both sides fought in the dark as well as the Generals: the English were, naturally victorious.

2. *The Siege of Sir Pastobol* (the memorable Russian General) who was quite besieged, and the English were very victorious.

3. *The Battle of Balaclava*, famous for the Charge of the Fire Brigade by Lord Tennyson and 599 other gallant men who, armed with Cardigans and Balaclava helmets, advanced for a league and a half (4½ miles), and back (9 miles), with the object of proving that someone had thundered the wrong order. (In which they were completely successful.)

4. *Flora MacNightshade*. The troops in the Crimea suffered terribly from their Cardigans and Balaclava helmets and from a new kind of overcoat invented by Lord Raglan, the Commander-in-Chief. They were also only allowed to wear boots on their left feet until the memorable intervention of Flora MacNightlight (the Lady with the Deadly Lamp-shade), who gave them boots for their right feet and other comforts, and cured them of their sufferings every night with doses of deadly lampshade.

'Flora MacNightlight'

'Suffered terribly from their Cardigans and Balaclava helmets'

CHAPTER LIV

THE INDIAN MUTINY

THIS was also inevitable on account of:

(a) *The Natives*. These believed that the English were going to make them bite their greasy cartileges (Chuputti). This they treacherously believed to be contrary to their religion and therefore a Bad Thing.

(b) *The Anglo-Indian*. The natives were unable to realize that these were a Good Thing.

Consequently an outbreak of very serious Meeruts occurred at Cawnpore and elsewhere and a descendant of the Great Mohawk was set up as Emperor at Dulwich (the old capital of India). Most terrible among the Indian leaders was a native Pundit called the Banana Sahib who by means of his treacherous disguise lured the famished British regiments to destruction.

The Mutiny, however, was a Good Thing as it was the cause of Lucknow being relieved by Generals Havelock, Ellis, etc., and Lord Roberts got the V.C. and stayed on for 41 years.

The Results of the Mutiny were:

(a) The Sepoy (or Governor-General) of India was brought under the control of the Crown.

(b) The Queen was declared to be the Great Mohawk of India.

CHAPTER LV

'PAL'

MEANWHILE, at home, fresh attempts to galvanize the Queen resulted in the promotion of Lord Palmerston ('Pal') to the Premiership – a rather matey minister who always wore green gloves and sucked a straw and altered the Despatches after the Queen had signed them, so that they became surprises for her. It was not, however, until he conceived and carried through his heartless *Conspiracy to Murder Bill* that the Good (but now Horrified) Queen dismissed him. After which 'Pal' spent his time taking special trains in all directions and galloping to Harrow on a cream-coloured pony, thus endearing himself to the People and becoming an object of terror and admiration to all foreign governments.

'Lord Palmerston ("Pal")'

CHAPTER LVI

FRESH ATTEMPTS TO AMUSE THE QUEEN. WAVE OF JUSTIFIABLE WARS

OWING to the inability of the Queen's ministers to amuse the Crown, superhuman attempts were now made by her Majesty's generals at home and abroad to provide military diversions. These took the form of a wave of justifiable Wars, including:

'Importation of Empire Opium into China'

1. *War with China*. Fought on moral grounds, because the Chinese government were disposed to impede the importation of Empire Opium into China. The British thus became indispensable to the Chinese and, after several bloody engagements, Hong Kong, the best port of China, was ceded to the British Throne.

2. *War with Afghanistan*. Owing to the size, direction, etc., of Russia, it was imperative that the King of Afghanistan, whose name was Just Mohammed, should sit on his throne in a friendly attitude. The King, however, (Just) declined to do this and the British Army was cut to pieces in the Pippa Passes to such an extent that Dr Brydle rode half alive (or, according to some historians, half dead) into Jallalla-ballad. After this, however, several bloody battles were fought, and the Kings of Afghanistan were compelled to sit in a more friendly attitude.

3. *Sheikh War*. Cause: Death of Ranji Tsinji (a huge Sheikh). The Sheikhs were very tall men on the frontier of India who obscured the Imperial outlook. A bloody strife ensued. Sir Hew Golf annihilated the Sheikhs, subsequently compelling them to present the Queen with a huge pencil called the Koh-in-Oor. The Sheikhs were thus reduced in every way and were afterwards on our side and a Good Thing.

4. *2nd Burmese War.* Cause: there had only been one Burmese war. Burmese cut to pieces. Burma ceded to the Crown. Peace with Burma.

5. *War against Abyssinia.* Object: to release the Europeans in Abyssinia, all of whom had been incarcerated by the King, Theodore, who was a Christian and would not see their point of view. The war was divided into two parts (1) Sir Robert Rapier demands release of prisoners. Prisoners released. (2) War declared against Abyssinia. King Theodore blown up with Magnesia, the capital of Abyssinia. Theodore commits suicide. Sir Robert becomes Lord Rapier of Magnesia. Peace with Abyssinia.

6. *War against A Shantee.* Coffee, King of a Shantee, worsted and burnt by Sir Garment Wolsee, who becomes Viscount Coffee. Peace with the Shantee.

7. *War against Zulus.* Cause: the Zulus. Zulus exterminated. Peace with Zulus.

'Object: to release the Europeans in Abyssinia'

*'Her Majesty's lip was
observed to tremble'*

All these attempts having failed, news was brought to the Queen that the Fiji Islands were annexed to the British 'by the desire of the inhabitants'. At this point, according to some (seditious) historians, Her Majesty's lip was observed to tremble.

SPHERES OF INTERFERENCE. EGYPT

It was during these wars that Spheres of Interference were discovered: these were necessary in all Countries inhabited by their own natives.

The first of the Spheres was Egypt which now became memorable for the first time since Potiphar, the well-known Egyptian Pharaoh.

Egypt was put under the Duel Control of England and France and was thus declared bankrupt; Alibaba, the Mowhgli, and other Pasha-Beziques were therefore immediately exterminated by Sir Garment Wolsey and subsequently by Kitchener of Kartoon at the terrible French battle of Homme de Man. This was because of Chinese Gordon (leader of the famous Gordon Riots* in Pekin) and was called the Pagoda Incident and is remarkable as being the only (memorable) *Incident* in History.

CHAPTER LVII

DISRAELI AND GLADSTONE

NOT very much is known about these two extremely memorable ministers, except that (a) *Disraeli* 'brought back Peace with Honour' after the famous Balkan Treaty of Berlin, which said:

1. that Bosnia should be ceded to Herzegovina;
2. that Herzegovina should be ceded to Bosnia (This is called the Eastern Question);

---

* Due to the justifiable looting of Pekin by the Allies.

'A romantic minister'

3. that Bulgaria should be divided into two parts
   (Later, Bulgaria was re-divided into one part by Mr
   Gladstone);

4. that anyone found in Armenia should be gradually
   divided into twelve parts. (Mr Gladstone subsequently criticised the effect of this clause.)

Disraeli also very generously purchased the Panama Canal from the Khalif and presented it to Queen Victoria with a huge bunch of primroses (his favourite flower), thus becoming Lord Beaconsfield and a romantic minister. The Queen, however, remained obdurately plural and not amused, even when Disraeli romantically called her a Faery Queen.

'Gladstone became angrier and angrier'

(*b*)   Gladstone, on the other hand, endeavoured (quite unsuccessfully) to please Her Majesty by chewing a milk pudding 79 times every day, and by his memorable inventions; amongst the latter were an exceptionally uncomfortable collar which he inhabited for 62 years on the floor of the House of Commons, and an extremely simple kind of bag which he designed to enable the Turks to be driven out of Europe *Bag and Baggage*. Gladstone also invented the Education Rate by which it was possible to calculate how soon anybody could be educated, and spent his declining years trying to guess the answer to the Irish Question; unfortunately, whenever he was getting warm, the Irish secretly changed the Question, so that as he grew older and older Gladstone became angrier and angrier, and grander and grander, and was ultimately awarded the affectionate title of 'the G.P.O.' Gladstone was thus clearly a Good Man but a Bad Thing (or, alternatively, a Bad Man but a Good Thing).

QUEEN VICTORIA'S JAMBOREE

Finally, all attempts (even by Gladstone and Disraeli) to amuse her, and to prevent her being good, having failed, the Queen held a Jamboree in Westminster Abbey and Crowned Heads and Oriental Patentees from all parts of the world came to acknowledge publicly the Good Queen's Victory over all her ministers and generals.

CHAPTER LVIII

THE BOERWOER

THE last event in Queen Victoria's reign was the Borewore, or, more correctly, Boerwoer (Dutch), which was fought against a very tiresome Dutch tribe called the Bores, because they were left over from all previous wars.

The War was not a very successful one at first, and was quite unfair because the Boers could shoot much further than the English, and also because they were rather despicable in wearing veldt hats and using Pom-Pom bullets.

'Rather despicable in wearing veldt hats'

Numerous battles were fought against the Bore leaders (such as Bother, Kopje, and Stellenbosch) at Nek's Creek, Creek's Nek, Knock's Knee, etc., and much assistance was given to the British cause by Strathcoma's memorable horse (patriotically lent by Lord Strathcoma for the occasion) and by the C.I.D., who fought very bravely and were awarded a tremendous welcome on their return to London after the war.

Finally, the people at home took upon themselves the direction of the War and won it in a single night in London by a new and bracing method of warfare known as *Mafeking*. Thus the English were once more victorious.

MEMORABLE RESULTS

The Barwar was obviously a Good Thing in the end because it was the cause of Boy Scouts and of their memorable Chief Scout, General Baden Powell (known affectionately as 'the B.O.P.'), and also because it gave rise to a number of very manly books, such as *40 Years Beating About The Bush, 50 Years Before The Mast, 60 Years Behind The Times*, etc.

'Naughty nineties'

DEATH OF QUEEN VICTORIA

Meanwhile Queen Victoria had celebrated another Jamboree, called the Diamond Jamboree (on account of the

discovery of Diamond mines at Camberley during the Borewore) and after dying of a surfeit of Jamborees, Jokes, Gladstone, etc., had been succeeded by her son, Edward VII.

CHAPTER LIX

WAVE OF INVENTIONS

'The Oxford Movement'

THE reign of Queen Victoria was famous for the numerous discoveries and inventions which happened in it. One of the first of these was the brilliant theory of Mr Darwin propounded in his memorable works, *Tails of a Grandfather, The Manx Man, Our Mutual Friends*, etc. This was known as Elocution or the Origin of Speeches and was fiercely denounced in every pulpit.

Another memorable invention was called the Oxford Movement: this was a form of sinuflection which led men gradually in the direction of Rome; the movement was first made by Cardinal Newton at Oxford, and later, Peeble and Pusey Colleges were found there to commemorate his assistants. Many illustrated manuals and pamphlets were written by Cardinals Newton and Peeble, giving directions for the movement.

There was also in Queen Victoria's reign a famous inventor and poet called Oscar Wilde who wrote very well but behaved rather beardsley; he made himself memorable by inventing Art, Ascesticism, etc., and was the leader of a set of disgusting old gentlemen called 'the naughty nineties'.

But most memorable of all were the McCanical inventions of the age, nearly all of which were kinds of Progress and invented by Scotsmen and Bad Things. Amongst these were Bicycles which caused Tricycles, coasting, bloomers, etc., and Roads (invented by Lord Macadam and his son Lord Tarmac) for them to go along. Other inventions were Thermometers (invented by Lord Farqualqhounheit) which caused Temperatures, inflolqhouenza, etc.;

'Wrote very well but . . .'

'Addicted to entente cordials, married a Sea-King's daughter, and invented appendicitis'

Telegrams which caused betting, Bismark, etc.; Mackintoshes (invented by another Scottish nobleman whose name is now forgotten); and the memorable line invented by Mr Plimsoll (see diagram below).

Most of these inventions, however, were too numerous to be mentioned.

Mr Plimsoll's Invention

CHAPTER LX

EDWARD VII, ALMOST A MONARCH

EDWARD VII was quite old when he came to the throne, but this was only on account of Queen Victoria, and he was really a very active man and had many romantic occupations; for instance, he went betting and visited Paris and was sometimes late for dinner; in addition he was merry with actresses and kind to gypsies.

Besides all this Edward VII smoked cigars, was addicted to entente cordials, married a Sea-King's daughter, and invented appendicitis. Edward VII was thus a very Good King, besides being a Good Thing and *amused* and, in fact, almost a *Monarch*. He is also memorable because he preferred making peace instead of war.

CHAPTER LXI

THE GREAT WAR

K ING EDWARD'S new policy of peace was very successful and culminated in the Great War to End War. This pacific and inevitable struggle was undertaken in the reign of His Good and memorable Majesty King George V and it was the cause of nowadays and the end of History.

CAUSES OF THE GREAT WAR

The Great War was between Germany and America and was thus fought in Belgium, one of the chief causes being the murder of the Austrian Duke of Sarajevo by a murderer in Servia.

There were many other Causes of the Great War, such as

1. German Governesses, a wave of whom penetrated Kensington in King Edward's reign and openly said that Germany ought to be top nation, and
2. The Kaiser who sent a telegram consisting entirely of ems to one of the memorable Boerwar leaders.*

These are now agreed to have been causes of the War though at the time the newspapers (rather conceitedly) declared that it was caused by a *strip of paper*.

---

*   And, during a subsequent crisis, a panther to Agaçiers (a brutal act and quite contrary to the Haig Convention).

THE WAR

The War lasted three years or the duration, the Americans being 100 per cent victorious. At the beginning the Russians rendered great assistance to the American cause by lending their memorable steam-roller and by passing silently through England one Sunday morning before breakfast with snow on their boots. The Americans were also assisted by the Australians (AZTECS) and some Canadians, and 51 Highlanders.

THE PEACE TO END PEACE

Though there were several battles in the War, none were so terrible or costly as the Peace which was signed afterwards in the ever-memorable Chamber of Horrors at Versailles, and which was caused by the only memorable American statesman, President Wilson and Col. White House, who insisted on a lot of Points, including

1. that England should be allowed to pay for the War: this was a Good Thing because it strengthened British (and even American) credit;
2. that the world should be made safe for democracy i.e. anyone except pillion-riders, pedestrians, foreigners, natives, capitalists, communists, Jews, riffs, R.A.F.S., gun-men, policemen, peasants, pheasants, Chinese, etc.;
3. that there should be a great many more countries: this was a Bad Thing as it was the cause of increased geography;
4. the Freedom of the Seas: this was a Good Thing as it did not apply to Britain or America (or Switzerland);
5. that the Kaiser should be hanged; this was a Good Thing as it was abandoned, together with Mr Lloyd George, the Irish Question, etc.

'Assisted by the Australians'

CHAPTER LXII

A BAD THING

MERICA was thus clearly top nation, and History came to a .

TEST PAPER V

UP TO THE END OF HISTORY

1. Sketch vaguely, with some reference to the facts: (1) The Southsea Bubble, (2) The Ramillies Wig.
2. Would it have been a Good Thing if Wolfe had succeeded in writing Gray's Elegy instead of taking Quebec?
3. Analyse and distinguish between the Begums of Oudh. Would they have been deceived by the Banana Sahib?
4. 'An Army marches on its stomach' (Napoleon). Illustrate and examine.
5. Account (loudly) for the success of Marshal Ney as a leader of horse.
6A. 'What a city to boot!' Who said this, Wellington or Blücher or Flora McNightingown?
6B. Did anybody say 'I know that no one can save this country and that nobody else can'? If not, who did say it?
7. Ruminate fearlessly on (1) Lord Cardigan, (2) Clapham.
8. Do not attempt to remember what Mr Gladstone said in 1864 but account for the paramountcy of (1) Milk Puddings, (2) Bags, in his political career.
9. Comment *Quietly* on
   (a) Tariff Reform.
   (b) Mafeking Night.
   (c) The Western Front.
10. Refrain from commencing on The Albert Memorial, The September Massacres, The Dardanelles, The O.B.E., or any other subjects that you consider too numerous to mention. (The better the fewer.)
11. Write not more than two lines on The Career of Napoleon Buonaparte, *or* The Acquisition of our Indian Empire *or* The Prime Ministers of England.
12. What price Glory?

N.B. – Do not on any account attempt to write on both sides of the paper at once.